D1231616

"We need more books like this to equip worship leaders effectively!" That was my response while reading *The Way of Worship*. The book is biblically sound, providing a solid theological foundation for those who are called to worship ministry. Michael Neale and Vernon M. Whaley elaborate on timeless and timely topics by skillfully blending insightful (and enjoyable) illustrations, practical guidance, and theological truths. This is a must-read not only for worship leaders but also for all followers of Christ who desire to understand true worship and deepen their worship of God. I look forward to using this as a textbook to train my Worship Studies students.

—**Jon Choi,** director of MA in Worship Studies and MA in Christian Ministry, Dallas Baptist University

"We are not the main character. Jesus is." I've been singing and leading worship for forty years, and this book challenged me and reminded me of why I do what I do! Michael and Dr. Whaley have painted a beautiful picture of what it means to be a true, submissive, confident worshiper of God. And don't you dare keep this book to yourself—pass it on and equip a fellow passenger on their incredible journey of worshiping our Savior!

—**Andy Chrisman,** worship leader, Dove Award–winning artist, internationally syndicated radio host

I am grateful to call Michael Neale a friend, and I am blessed to serve this generation of the body of Christ alongside him. His voice is one that I trust, and I am excited to see this new resource, *The Way of Worship*, teach, inspire, and bring revelation to a new generation of worship leaders.

—**Travis Cottrell,** worship leader, Living Proof Live with Beth Moore

Michael Neale is a gift to the church in our generation. The integrity of his life and ministry speaks to a new generation of worship leaders—including pastors and all who serve Christ. In this significant book, you will discover a biblical pathway for true worship starting with the spiritual vitality of those who lead and leading to a fresh encounter with Jesus. *The Way of Worship* is destined to become a classic read for all who desire to discover the presence and power of God in worship.

—**Dr. Jack Graham,** senior pastor, Prestonwood
Baptist Church, Plano, Texas

This engaging story of a river journey combined with Biblical truth engages the reader in experiencing the spirit and truth of genuine worship and their journey with Christ. Michael Neale and Vernon Whaley give the reader excellent tools for nurturing the inward journey of spiritual growth.

—**Sam Green, EdD,** chair, Department of
Worship, Trevecca Nazarene University

Before going somewhere I've never been, I want to talk to someone who has been there—someone with credible experience. With *The Way of Worship*, that is precisely what we have—a journey down the tributaries of worship in Scripture, all the way to a river of wonders in the presence of God, led by two travelers who know the journey well. What's more, they give us their story from the vantage point of God's Word. Neale and Whaley serve us powerfully as the "Lewis and Clark" of what God's Word says about worship. You will love this journey and be challenged along the way!

—**Mike Harland,** director, LifeWay Worship

Michael Neale and Dr. Vernon Whaley are two of the most respected voices on worship and music in the church. I am so excited about their new book, *The Way of Worship*. This book is a gift to the body of Christ! I truly believe this book is a must-have for every worship pastor, worship leader, and worship team member.

—**Mark Harris,** award-winning songwriter/artist,
worship pastor, Gateway Church, Southlake, Texas

With compelling stories, practical applications, and insights that come from years of experience in joining their deep personal faith with local church expressions, Michael and Vernon take us on a delightful journey of renewing our call, sharpening our focus, and centering our goal of guiding others in worship.

—**Stephen P. Johnson, DMA,** dean, College
of the Arts, Azusa Pacific University

Filled with the sacred narrative of God's love for us and powerful, practical worship theology, Michael and Dr. Whaley give laser focus to what it means and what it takes to be a worship leader in the modern church. This book provides everything needed to encourage and sustain worship leaders in their important role!

—**John Larson,** worship pastor, Church of the
Highlands, Birmingham, Alabama

Michael Neale is one of the most creatively gifted storytellers I know. His songs, stories, and leadership have impacted countless people. In this engaging and comprehensive study, Michael and Vernon guide us deep into the waters of worship to experience God and his Word in a unique and powerful way.

—**Dr. Tom Mullins,** founding pastor, Christ
Fellowship Church, Palm Beach Gardens, Florida

The Way of Worship is a refreshing look at what it means to be a worshiper. Using the metaphor of whitewater river rafting, Pastor Neale guides us into thinking about the metaphor's application to worship, and Dr. Whaley underpins the application with further biblical focus. This results in each chapter being a modern worship parable with solid biblical teaching to support and expound upon it. It will be a highly recommended book for my students!

—**Roger O'Neele,** associate professor of
worship, Cedarville University

With the perfect blend of story, metaphor, and practical application, *The Way of Worship* is not just a book you read; it's a road map that helps you discover the very essence of what it means to be a worship leader. This resource is incredibly helpful in rediscovering the "why" behind what we do. It's something the church needs today more than ever. I believe that the truth found in these pages will bring you clarity and passion and will unlock a greater power for you and your teams. It's a must-read for worship leaders.

—**Drew Powell,** creative arts pastor, Cross
Point Church, Nashville, Tennessee

Neale and Whaley capture the call to worship through compelling story and reflection. *The Way of Worship* conveys an all-encompassing journey of faith in which every aspect of life and purpose becomes a glorious response to Christ. This work is a devotional joy! I recommend it for personal growth and ministry in the local church.

—**Dr. Paul Rumrill,** associate dean, Center for
Music and Worship, Liberty University

In their practical and insightful book, *The Way of Worship*, Michael Neale and Dr. Vernon Whaley have given us an excellent guide—a road map—for worship. This book is an invaluable resource for those who plan and lead worship. Follow it and your congregations will be blessed with a deeper, more meaningful experience of worship.

—**Rory Noland,** director of Heart of the Artist Ministries, director of Worship Studies, Hope International University and Nebraska Christian College

There is no higher calling or greater responsibility than leading others to engage actively in the worship of a holy God. In *The Way of Worship: A Guide to Living and Leading Authentic Worship*, my friend and worship pastor, Michael Neale, will lead you on a journey of discovering what genuine worship is as well as offer practical insight and advice to those serving in this unique role. The church needs leaders today that are humble in spirit, excellent in skill, and driven to seek the glory of God above all. That is who Michael Neale is, and that is why you can follow this guide he and Dr. Whaley have written. I recommend it to anyone who desires to worship God in "spirit and in truth."

—**Dr. Jarret Stephens,** teaching pastor, Prestonwood Baptist Church

The Way of Worship is a fresh and powerful resource for worship leaders. Incredible storytelling and deep wisdom flow in this engaging work. My friends Michael Neale and Vernon Whaley have captured something special to guide a generation of worshipers to live and lead authentic, Jesus-centered worship. I highly recommend it!

—**Michael W. Smith,** singer/songwriter

Michael is not only a powerfully anointed worship leader; he is a friend. His giftedness flows from the character and integrity of his heart. He and Dr. Vernon Whaley have spread out a map and an irresistible call for the worshiping church for years to come.

—**Shelia Walsh,** author of *Praying Women*

If there is a textbook for Worship 101, this is it. Michael Neale and Dr. Vernon Whaley have written a book that is incredibly straightforward yet exceptionally profound. *The Way of Worship* will no doubt prove to be a priceless resource for those longing to be people who worship in spirit and in truth. In a world that is struggling to rediscover its wonder and sense of awe, I highly recommend this book to the church leader and churchgoer alike.

—**Darren Whitehead,** lead pastor, Church of the City, Nashville, Tennessee, coauthor of *Holy Roar: 7 Words That Will Change The Way You Worship* (with Chris Tomlin)

What Michael Neale and Dr. Vernon Whaley have penned is a mustread for those of us in worship and church leadership. Unfolding the essence of worship through the practical lens of a nature-filled journey reinforces the belief that God is indeed everywhere and in everything. I believe this book will serve as a manual to many seeking a deeper understanding of the practice, performance, and posture of a worshiper and leader.

—**Dr. Oscar Williams Jr.,** executive director of arts and music, the Potter's House and T. D. Jakes Ministries

THE WAY OF
WORSHIP

THE WAY OF
WORSHIP

A GUIDE TO LIVING AND LEADING
AUTHENTIC WORSHIP

MICHAEL NEALE AND
VERNON M. WHALEY

ZONDERVAN®

ZONDERVAN

The Way of Worship
Copyright © 2020 by Michael Neale and Vernon M. Whaley

Requests for information should be addressed to:
Zondervan, *3900 Sparks Dr. SE, Grand Rapids, Michigan 49546*

ISBN 978-0-310-10404-9 (hardcover)

ISBN 978-0-310-10405-6 (ebook)

Published in association with Verne Kenney.

Cover design: Micah Kandros
Cover art: Shutterstock®
Interior design: Kait Lamphere

Printed in the United States of America

20 21 22 23 24 25 26 27 28 29 30 /LSC/ 17 16 15 14 13 12 11 10 9 8 7 6 5 4 3 2 1

*To all the worship leaders and pastors who
faithfully guide people day after day, week after
week, to respond to the majesty and wonder of
Jesus in full-hearted, life-surrendered worship*

CONTENTS

PART 2: PRACTICES
C. HIS POWER, OUR AWARENESS

D. HIS WORK, OUR RELATIONSHIPS

FOREWORD

The Word of God is the only source we can use to gain a true understanding of the realities of worship. The second book of the Bible describes one of the most epic events in Scripture: the exodus of the Hebrews from Egypt. Since the Hebrews lived in slavery, one might expect that the overriding purpose of the exodus must be freedom from oppression and bondage. Not so! God instructed Moses: "Go to Pharaoh and say to him, 'This is what the Lord says: Let my people go, *so that they may worship me*'" (Exod 8:1). Throughout the exodus narrative, Moses repeats that powerful message from the Lord. The ultimate purpose of deliverance from Egyptian rule was freedom to worship the Hebrew God, YHWH.

Scottish Olympic gold medalist Eric Liddell, portrayed so well in the 1981 movie *Chariots of Fire*, said, "God made me fast. And when I run, I feel his pleasure." Hearing him say that in the movie struck a chord with me. In the years that followed, I've been reminded of Eric's powerful statement as I step up to a microphone, readying to lead believers in worship. To be honest, I always begin from a place of trepidation and anxiety. But after I've sung the first few lines, I move to a place of peace. It's hard to explain where this anxiety originates.

Sometimes it comes from knowing my own shortcomings or from feeling unworthy to lead others in worship. Other times I'm afraid that the people in the room may not want to join in and worship. Once I forget my worries and abandon myself to worshiping the Lord, regardless of the people in the room or the voices in my head, I feel peace. It never fails, even after having done this for well over thirty years. And when I'm in the middle of a worship song, singing together with other believers, I also "feel his pleasure."

In this age, we are surrounded by a culture that worships everything but God (Rom 1:25). Oh, how we have lost our way! You and I are not immune to the temptation to place other things before worshiping God. We need constant reminders to focus on him and not to be enticed by the distractions around us.

Getting to a place of peace is something I desire. Unfortunately, it doesn't come automatically; I have to pursue it. The social media channels vying for my attention are invariably filled with vitriol. Truth is replaced by opinion, peace by angst, acceptance by suspicion, love for God and others by ego and self-gratification.

The last thing I want in a book about worship is someone's opinion. That is why this new narrative by Michael Neale and Vernon Whaley is so refreshing and timely. Using an inspiring whitewater rafting experience as a canvas, Michael skillfully draws parallels between the difficulties of navigating a wild, unpredictable, and dangerous river and the spiritual lessons learned while leading worship and serving the church. Then, almost immediately, I am drawn to Scripture and theology. And the Holy Spirit transforms an engaging story into a personal worship encounter. I find the book devoid of personal opinion and rich with insight that benefits me as one called into the worship ministry.

The life of every believer is filled with pitfalls and temptations, but I dare say that for those whose ministry involves speaking, teaching, or leading worship, the dangers can be unique. James 3:1 warns us: "Not many of you should become teachers, my fellow believers, because you know that we who teach will be judged more strictly." For those in public ministry, vigilance is required if we desire to maintain a humble posture, something the authors of this book cover so well in the chapters on brokenness and humility.

Use this book with your worship team. Laboring together with your team is like working out in a spiritual gym. Rather than getting your physical body in shape, spiritual workouts constantly challenge us to forgive, submit, practice patience, encourage, and serve one another. Worship teams provide opportunities for every team member to grow in maturity. And make sure to study and implement the chapters on unifying and collaboration too because they provide key insights for growth.

In the years since I started leading worship at our small East Texas congregation with simple guitar and vocals, modern worship music has grown into a major part of the church experience, and an entire industry has sprung up to support it. Much of it is to be applauded, and most of the time I am tempted to call it "progress." But sometimes, when I see people spend a lot of time and resources on amazing equipment and the latest technologies, I begin to worry and remember the story of Gideon. He started with an army of 32,000 men, but it wasn't until the Lord told him to bring that number down to 300 men that God brought the victory—lest anyone should boast. So occasionally, when we feel the pendulum swing too far, we should look for a balance. My friend and occasional cowriter Matt Redman so beautifully described his difficulty with the direction everything seemed to be going when he wrote:

> I'm coming back to the heart of worship
> And it's all about you,
> It's all about you, Jesus.
> I'm sorry, Lord, for the thing I've made it.

The Way of Worship takes us on a journey of discovering what spirit-led worship creates in us and in the teams we have the privilege of leading. Michael's insightful analogies and Vernon's scriptural underpinnings help provide an inspirational new focus on this important and eternal activity, one I have dedicated my life to. May the chapters that follow be an inspiration and guide to you, and may you "feel his pleasure" as you worship him.

Paul Baloche

INTRODUCTION

Guide (Merriam-Webster definition)

- A person who leads or directs other people on a journey
- A person who shows and explains the interesting things in a place

It was the summer of 1997, and we were celebrating my sweetheart's graduation from college. Leah and I saved our pennies and decided to embark on an adventure to the Colorado Rockies for some hiking, sightseeing, and whitewater rafting.

That crisp June morning, we stumbled into the old red house that doubled as an outpost for the rafting company. A weathered, grey-bearded outdoorsman busy shuffling papers and clipboards on the reclaimed wood counter greeted us. Imagine Jeff Bridges, and you'll have a pretty good idea.

Just a few moments later, a tan, blond, bushy-haired Adonis appeared through the rickety screen door off the back porch. His muscle shirt revealed a chiseled torso. He was toweling off his hands as he entered and made his way over to us. I immediately had mixed emotions. Emotion #1: *Whew, I'm glad this is our guide. He looks legit.* Emotion #2: *Perfect. I'm a scrawny, newly married Barney Fife, and our guide looks like Thor.*

He greeted us confidently. He seemed kind, generous . . . magnetic even. We were laughing immediately, like old friends. Just talking to these men made us feel like we were being drawn into another world.

John (which, it turned out, was Thor's real name) and his apprentice, Anastasia, a thickset Swede who doubled as a ski instructor during the winter, got us each fitted for a wetsuit, helmet, and PFD (personal flotation device). About that time, a gigantic balding man stepped through a sliding barn door.

"Are we gonna get friggin' wet or what?" he bellowed in his boisterous Brooklyn accent. "Hey Franny, let's do 'dis."

In walked a pocket-sized woman with heels, painted-on acid wash jeans, and teased out blonde hair reminiscent of 1980s glam.

"Neal, if I chip a nail, or get this hair wet, you . . . are dead . . . to me." The little New Yorker pointed her chubby finger at him.

"Oh, this is gonna be good," John said flashing a huge smile as he checked the fit of my helmet. We were all laughing hysterically.

After about forty minutes of driving and small talk, the rusty fifteen-passenger van carried us off the winding mountain highway onto a narrow unpaved path, revealing a heart-stopping view. A misty fog hovered over the gently moving river. The red rock canyon walls rose hundreds of feet into the air. The fragrant spruce and fir trees stood at attention along the river, and a regal hawk nested high in the cliff watched over us like a guardian. The river was majestic, wide, and mysterious.

We piled into our faded-blue raft and took our places on each section of the tubes: Neal and I in the front, Leah and Franny in the middle, Anastasia and John in the very back. As John began to explain the commands he would call to unite our paddling, my heart thumped. He discussed our safety at great length and the adventurous perils that lay ahead as we rotated slowly through the magnificent canyon.

At that moment, the trip became *real* to me. This wasn't some pleasant outing to the park. We were entering the wild. There was no turning back. We were doing something beautiful . . . something unpredictable . . . something dangerous . . . and truly incredible.

The events of that one-day journey on the river are still reverberating in my life all these years later. It has inspired me—someone who struggled in school with literature and comprehension—to write novels, musical compositions, and theatrical scripts. It spawned an education foundation for at-risk youth. It is the wellspring of dozens of talks and lessons I've shared as a leader and pastor for groups and conferences. And it has ignited the study that I'm passing on to you in this labor of love.

Leading worship has been at the core of my calling for the better part of twenty-five years—ministering to the Savior in music and inviting people to join in the adoration song of the ages to Jesus, the Lamb of God who takes away the sins of the world.

There are striking parallels between what our whitewater guide John did that day in *guiding* us to experience the grandeur and majesty of the river and the role of worship leaders. In fact, I like to call them *worship guides*, because it emphasizes their calling to help others experience the power and presence of the Almighty in surrendered, full-life worship.

John was the ultimate rafting guide because he helped us understand that *the river is the center of everything.*

I (Michael) and my dear friend and worship-theologian Dr. Vernon M. Whaley are inviting you to join us on a daring journey into the Holy Scriptures. Each chapter begins with a brief episode of a story inspired by our real-life journey on the river that day. (Names have been changed and some details embellished for effect.) We will uncover new connections between our experiences on the river and the role of worship leaders by plumbing the depths of God's Word to sharpen our minds, quicken our spirits, and learn the way of worship

I (Vernon) am also excited to share with you during this journey together. It is my joy to make biblical application to the narrative so skillfully crafted by Michael Neale. We are using "the river" as a metaphor for the calling God has placed on our lives through Jesus Christ. These "river" sections will be indicated by the river icon above, just as the story sections at the beginning of each chapter are designated by a quill icon. In some traditions, water or rivers have symbolized the working of the Holy Spirit in the life of the believer. For us, we are using the river to represent the person of God himself as Father, Son (Jesus Christ), and the Holy Spirit.

Why a river? Rivers in Scripture often hold important insights about God, redemption, and worship. In Genesis the word *river* appears for the first time in the Bible. The Bible goes into great detail to describe perfect worship with a perfect God in a perfect place, the Garden of Eden. The author specifically points out that a river flowed through Eden and watered the garden. Why might that be?

There are many other important rivers throughout the scriptural narrative. There are no less than 148 references to a river or rivers involving God's plan for his people after the first river mentioned in Genesis 2:10. When God makes a covenant with Abram, he marks out the boundaries of the promised land by the river of Egypt and the Euphrates.[1] Moses's very name relates the story of how his mother saves his life by setting him afloat on the river in an ark of bulrushes.[2] Job drinks of the river water from the Jordan.[3] Psalm 1 compares a man who fears God to a tree planted by the river. Again, the psalmist compares God's provisions to a flowing river. Psalm 46 says there is a river that brings joy to the heavenly city, where the true source of security is God himself.[4] The prophets Jeremiah, Ezekiel, Joel, and Daniel all employ rivers as metaphors for God's provision.[5] Zechariah and Daniel's visions include a river. Jesus was baptized in a river,[6] and he describes the Holy Spirit being like a river in the believer's heart.[7] The disciples baptized the first Christians in a river,[8] and Paul prays by the riverside.[9] John sees a pure river of water of life in his great eschatological vision described in Revelation.[10]

The river is a symbol of life. In Genesis, a river flows from Eden, the source of all life and relationships, and then splits into four different streams that water the nations. The river in heaven flows from the throne of God. Rivers represent God's provisions to sustain, love, and care for his own creation—including you and me.

This provision and relationship is what we will investigate throughout this book. Relationship with a Holy God, through Jesus Christ, is at the heart of our worship and the basis for our worship leading. So "the river is the center."

At the end of each chapter, I (Vernon) will also provide a "wisdom" section, targeting essential issues facing those of us leading worship every week. These wisdom sections are indicated by the book icon because the Scriptures are our primary source. Twenty-eight strategic "heart issues" are dealt with and discussed as they relate to the joy of worship. These sections will dig into God's Word to help us create a biblical frame for worship.

PART I: PRECEPTS

A. HIS REVELATION, OUR RESPONSE

CHAPTER 1

HIS PLAN

"There it is." John spoke reverently as he took one guiding stroke with his paddle.

"What? There what is?" Franny asked nervously.

It was eerily quiet as we began our journey. The first section of the river carried us gently through the serpentine bends of the canyon.

"Evidence."

"Evidence? Is it a bear?" With her strong accent, it sounded like "bee-ah." She smacked her gum mercilessly. "I knew it."

"Calm down. There ain't no bears out here. Geez!" Neal bellowed in his heavy Brooklyn cadence.

"It's all around us," John said. His squinting gaze scanned the magical world we were entering.

Franny furrowed her brow in bewilderment. If these initial minutes were any indication, she was going to use the most words on the trip.

John's at-times cryptic way of speaking made it feel as if we were dropping in on the middle of a conversation he was having with himself.

We sat silently as the raft coasted down the river. I was curious. "What are you referring to?" I asked.

"Look around. The beauty, the order, the majesty . . . I'll never get over it. Human hands didn't make this. This wasn't dreamed up in the mind of an earthling. I believe there's a maker. I don't always understand it, but I believe there's a plan."

"A plan?"

The guide ripped into a piece of beef jerky and talked through his chewing. "I don't believe in accidents. The canyon walls. The wildlife. The sky. The river and how it carves out the earth and brings life to the lowest places. Us. There's a plan for us. We are here with the river today, experiencing her in all her glory. We have a place in it all. There's evidence of a plan. A greater story."

The surroundings seemed to make poetic insight spill out of him, and it caught me by surprise.

"It's breathtaking," Leah commented. "We are a long way from the flatlands of Florida."

John flashed a coy grin. "You haven't seen anything yet, Leah."

I didn't like that he already knew my young wife's name.

He took one more bite, stuffed the remainder in his dry bag, and smiled again.

"Oh, and there are bears."

Lord, you are my God;
    I will exalt you and praise your name,
for in perfect faithfulness
    you have done wonderful things,
    things planned long ago.
        —ISAIAH 25:1

When you need to go somewhere, on a long trip for instance, and there's a map of how to get to your destination, you want to know it, right? That map—or more likely a GPS these days—is your guide to find your campground, make your way back to your family home, or explore a new countryside. Similarly, God has a plan for all of us: a journey to his heart and the purpose of why we are here.

> Remember the former things, those of long ago;
>> I am God, and there is no other;
>> I am God, and there is none like me.
> I make known the end from the beginning,
>> from ancient times, what is still to come.
> I say, "My purpose will stand,
>> and I will do all that I please."
>> —ISAIAH 46:9–10

The maker, as our guide John said, the sovereign Lord of heaven and earth who is outside of time and space, is working his plan. The one who was before the beginning and will be for all eternity is weaving all that exists into a beautiful tapestry. He is not surprised by anything. He is ahead, behind, above, and below. He knows all and sees all.

In his love and perfect knowledge, God's perfect design includes a plan for worship. It is a plan that directs our affections, our longings, and our desires, leading us to the only one who will satisfy us, heal us, deliver us, and save us from ourselves: Jesus.

> For in him all things were created: things in heaven and on earth, visible and invisible, whether thrones or powers or rulers or authorities; all things have been created through him and for him. He is before all things, and in him all things hold together.
>> —COLOSSIANS 1:16–17

This plan will cost us more than we ever thought we'd pay and fulfill us more than we ever dared dream. This plan is perfect. His plan for us to give ourselves in full-life, surrendered, serving, adoring worship is the very essence of why we are here. As the Westminster Catechism states, "The chief end of man is to glorify God and enjoy Him forever."

This is the way of worship.

> In the process of being worshiped . . .
> God communicates his presence to men.
> —C. S. LEWIS[1]

Welcome to the way of worship. Each chapter explores different aspects of worship and how worship leaders can approach their calling, both from a biblical and a personal perspective.

In the first half of the book, we will focus on discovering the biblical perspective on worship. The first seven chapters deal with our response to God's revelation and coming to understand God's plan, call, awesomeness, wonder, and revelation, and our responsibility to develop a spirit of gratitude. In chapters 8–14, attention is given to the relationship between God's purposes and our obedience. Leading worship isn't all about strategies and knowledge. We also have to confront issues of the heart like character, brokenness, humility, stewardship of time, integrity, and recognizing Jesus as the source for successful worship.

But in this first chapter, we will lay the groundwork for understanding God's plan for worship.

What does it mean "to glorify God and enjoy Him forever," and what does it even mean to "enjoy God"? These are critically important questions, and the answer can only be found in the source of life, God himself.

You see, the Lord of heaven and earth is strategic in *all* his ways. He is deliberate and intentional—you might even say tactical! He is a God of purpose and eternal design. And while I would never dare say that our God is a "type A" or "choleric" or any other human personality, he is a God of order, structure, and careful planning, carefully creating the earth and heavens for his creatures to live in. The Bible tells us that from before the foundations of this world began, God set in order a plan for all creation to love, enjoy, and find enormous satisfaction by being in his presence—the presence of an *almighty, majestic, wonderful* God.

But mere power isn't a reason to trust someone. He is also a God of love, compassion, kindheartedness, and benevolence. It is because of this *great love* that on the sixth day of creation this very "Eternal God scooped dirt out of the ground, sculpted it into the shape we call human, breathed the breath that gives life into the nostrils of the human, and the human became a living soul" (Gen 2:7 The Voice). It is that *living breath*, the very spirit of God, that makes every man, woman, boy, and girl an eternal being. It is that *spirit*, which we often call our "soul," that sets humanity apart from all the animals and other living creatures on this earth.

God is a God of *relationship*. At the very moment he formed man of the dust of the ground and breathed into his nostrils the breath of life, God placed deep inside humanity's spirit a fervent and breathtaking desire to worship. The God of the universe desires complete, full, and uninterrupted relationship with humanity, and this is accomplished in worship through the person of his Son, Jesus Christ. Nothing in the whole world will satisfy the longing to know and be known by God except worship of him.

God is also a God of *revelation*. From the beginning of time, our creator made a way for us to come to know him. We call this "revelation," his dynamic method for humanity to know, understand, and find God. God reveals himself to mankind through nature (Ps 8:3–4;

Job 26:8, 9, 14; Rom 1:20); our conscience (Rom 2:14–15); his Son, Jesus Christ (Heb 1:1–2; Matt 11:27; John 14:6–7, 11–13); and the Holy Bible (2 Tim 3:16).

Beginning with Genesis and the truth that God is the ultimate creator, and concluding with worship of "the Lamb" in Revelation, God reveals himself to humanity. And humanity's response to God's self-revelation is both wonderful and mysterious, which is why so many books, treatises, articles, sermons, and lectures have been written about it! Our response to God's revelation is worship of him with a sincere, honest, and contrite heart. Always!

God is a God of *redemption*. Through revelation, God makes known to us his free gift of salvation. Through Scripture, we learn about God's plan to redeem and glorify his children and dwell with them forever, without sin, anger, envy, sadness, malice, hatred, or any of the other evils that plague us now. He does this through his work on the cross, where Christ our redeemer carried out the mystery of salvation.

God's Plan for Worship

What is worship? How does man worship? How does worship of God shape my life? Why does God want us to worship in spirit and truth?

The Bible tells us that "long ago, even before he made the world, God chose us to be his very own through what Christ would do for us; he decided then to make us holy in his eyes, without a single fault—we who stand before him covered with his love. His unchanging plan has always been to adopt us into his own family by sending Jesus Christ to die for us. *And he did this because he wanted to*"—and because He loves us! (Eph 1:4–5 TLB; emphasis added).

And why did God want to do this? God desires that we should praise and give glory to him for doing these mighty things for us! (Eph 1:12).

Just as God's plan of redemption is outlined throughout Scripture, *his plan for worship* is defined and delineated in his Word. God's strategy and divine blueprint for worship parallels the grand, compassionate story of redemption. In the Old Testament, the story of worship is demonstrated through his mighty acts, power, and wonder. In the New Testament, the story of worship is explained (in the book of Hebrews) through the redemptive work of Jesus, our own, personal worship leader—our great high priest. And God's plan for worship is consummated in Revelation, where Jesus is worshiped as Lord of lords and King of kings.

So what does it mean to worship God? Jesus said, "Love the Lord your God with all your heart and with all your soul and with all your strength and with all your mind" (Luke 10:27)! To worship is to love God and to tell him that you love him.

God's plan for worship is perfect, personal, and powerful. The Bible tells us that God is love, and he plans and charts the way of his children. And God's pattern for worship involves practical application of revealed truth. The issues surrounding worship are important and life-changing. They impact every area of our lives—spiritual, emotional, relational, physical, and intellectual. Join us as we unpack life principles that open up the door for developing a vibrant worship relationship with God and a pathway for understanding the way of worship.

CHAPTER 2

HIS CALL

"Before we make this bend in the river, I need you to pay close attention. We're going to hit our first major rapid of the day," our guide said firmly.

"Is this where the fat New Yorker goes in the drink and drowns?" Neal's thick Brooklyn accent couldn't hide his nervousness.

"Not if you pay attention," John said with a coy grin.

Neal cocked his head toward Franny. "Why did you get us into this again?"

"Excuse me? Do you people hear this? I remind you big boy, *you* told me that an adventure was calling you. Maybe there was more than the concrete jungle, you said. Remember that?" she asked as she pointed her fake nail at him.

"Okay guys, we're going to have to settle this later," John said. "Forward hard!"

We snapped to attention quickly, our paddles in the water, and made our way around the bend into our first rapid. We accelerated, lunging up and down over the waves. The frigid whitewater splashed over the bow as our hearts raced. It was exhilarating. We slapped our paddles like a high-five, thrilled to have successfully navigated the foamy waters.

"Neal, you mentioned the adventure calling you," John said once things had quieted down. "Tell us more about that."

"I don't know. I just knew I needed a change of scenery. I wanted to experience something that wasn't man made, ya know? So I'm flippin' through this outdoor magazine and see these photos of these guys riding the whitewater, hiking in the mountains, all that. It just called to me. Then I had to convince little missy over there."

"Whatevah." Franny rolled her eyes. John smiled cryptically.

"The river called me, for sure," he said. "I belong to the waters. It's like the waters chose me to be here, to revel in the beauty and power, and to guide others to do the same. I couldn't really think about being anywhere else or doing anything else. Maybe that'll be you after this trip, Neal!"

"How many fat guides from New York do you have out here?" Neal quipped.

"You could be the first!" Everyone burst into laughter.

The river called me, for sure. I belong to the waters.

Have you ever felt a mysterious call like the one John described? God calls us to himself. The river of life beckons us. We belong to him. He calls us to relationship with him, to experience his love, forgiveness, and power, and he calls us to join him in the renewal of all things through our gifting and ministry. And just as John found fulfilment by answering the call he felt, there is no greater joy and purpose than answering the call to salvation and the call to life in ministry. It all begins with God's call. He initiates, and we respond.

I was nine years old in a small country church when I first heard God's loving call. Around seventy-five people had showed up to hear a traveling gospel-singing family perform at a Sunday night camp meeting service. The son and daughter sang, the mother played the piano, and the father preached.

The grace of God poured over me like a tidal wave that night. I sensed the Spirit of God say, "I love you, Michael. I made you, and I know you. I have a plan for you. Follow me." I really understood in those moments that I needed a Savior to forgive my sins. I knew I was made for something far greater than myself. And I sensed a call. But for me, the call wasn't to the river—it was to music ministry. The young family's music moved and inspired me to learn and create. I wasn't sure what it meant then, but it set me on the course for a life of guiding people to worship God and enjoy his presence primarily through sacred music. This call to ministry was confirmed over and over through Scripture, wise counsel, and my personal, God-given gifting.

His call brings us to salvation. His call brings us to relationship. His call brings us to our purpose. His call directs us to our ministry.

In Isaiah 6, we see the prophet have a glorious encounter with the Lord and receive a deep call of ministry and mission.

The river calls to us. We belong to the living waters.

> Then I heard the voice of the Lord saying, "Whom shall I send? And who will go for us?"
> And I said, "Here am I. Send me!"
> —ISAIAH 6:8

Understanding the call we feel drawing us is critical to those seeking the way of worship. Those serving as worship leaders must learn to identify, understand, and obey the call on their lives. Following the call defines success or failure in leading others into worship. It goes to the very core of the worshiper's being.

In the last section, we compared the call John felt "to revel in the beauty and power" of the river to guide others, to how Michael answered God's call to salvation and discern a call to music when he was nine years old.

God's call brings us to our purpose and to our ministry. What does this all mean for the worshiper? Like the word *worship*, *call* can be both a verb and a noun—an action and a thing. It involves doing and being.

A calling is a divine "setting apart" of the worshiper for a specific task. It is something you become. The word for "calling" in the Greek concordance of the Bible is *klēsis*. Only appearing eleven times in eleven verses of the New Testament, this kind of "calling" is a divine invitation to be treasured. *Calling involves an ever-deepening relationship with God,* not simply obligating one's self to a vocation or a task. Those being called have an innate understanding that God has a special claim and ownership on their lives.

But "call" is also something that someone does. It means being "summoned, called out, or called forth from something." It comes from the Greek word *kaléō,* which describes "bidding, wooing, or drawing" someone into an action. This word is used very intentionally and sparingly in the Bible. Only twenty-four times does this type of Greek rendering for the word *calling* appear in the entire New Testament.

This is the word used to describe Jesus calling his disciples and constant companions. Perhaps this shows us why calling is so very important.

First, the call is personal. God chooses the person individually, and it is only *his* decision. God is very selective in this calling process, as we see in 1 Corinthians 1:26: "Brothers and sisters, think of what you were when you were called. Not many of you were wise by human standards; not many were influential; not many were of noble birth."

Second, God's calling is a vital part of his purposes. His sovereign design is to call choice servants—just like you—and set them apart for strategic tasks, opportunities, and purposes.

God has placed a special calling upon your life! The Bible teaches that God chose us "in accordance with his pleasure and will—to the praise of his glorious grace" (Eph 1:4, 5–6). It also tells us he called us "before time began" (see 2 Tim 1:9).

Third, God's calling is a two-fold process. The one who is chosen must *recognize* and then *respond* to the call.

The call is not invented or based on job demand. It is a mystery revealed to the worshiper by God himself. In one true sense, God shapes the heart of the worshiper through the act of calling. God alone reveals the calling.

Once you recognize the call, you must respond to the call immediately. When God calls, the worshiper's responsibility is to obey without delay.

There is not a single formula for receiving God's call. Sometimes, God calls through circumstances or the encouragement of others. The call can come as a still, small voice or a dramatic revelation. Sometimes we only come to understand the call over a long time. But no matter how God chooses to communicate, the process is the same: recognize God's call, and respond with obedience.

When God calls Abraham from the heathen lands of Ur to a new promised land, Abraham responds immediately: "Here I am." He moves his family to a new land. When God calls again in Genesis 22, Abraham answers the call by offering his only son as a sacrifice with the same, simple response: "Here I am." And in the process God reveals himself to Abraham and Isaac as Jehovah Jireh. By faith, Abram obeys God. Why? Obedience is at the heart and core of worship (Gen 12:1–9; 15:7; Acts 7:2–4; Heb 11:8–12).

Moses comes face to face with God's call through a burning bush. His response is familiar to us: "Here I am."

Joshua hears the call of God. His immediate answer is "Here I am." In the process, God reveals to Joshua the "captain of the Lord's army."

Even as a child, Samuel knew how to respond to God's call (in 1 Sam 3) with: "Here I am."

And Isaiah, when answering the call centuries later (Isa 6), used the same words: "Here I am."

Jesus responds most vividly in the garden to the call of the cross by praying, "Not my will but Thine be done."

And Paul, on the Damascus road, recognizes God's call, miraculously responds with intentional obedience, and enjoys an ever-deepening relationship with Christ.

God's call is *powerful* and *persistent*. I cannot receive God's calling on your behalf. You must answer the call yourself—personally, individually. The calling comes directly from God. And you cannot fulfill a call God has issued to me. Speaking of Jesus, the apostle Paul writes,

> Who has saved us and *called* us [verb = action] with a holy *calling* [noun = title], not according to our works, but according to His own purpose and grace which was given to us in Christ Jesus before time began.
>
> —2 TIMOTHY 1:9 NASB; EMPHASIS ADDED

This is a promise for those who answer the call. In our story, John confesses, "I couldn't really think about being anywhere else or doing anything else." John's heart draws him to the water. Nothing satisfies John like being in and around this body of water. John is the only one in the boat with the call to the river. The draw and commitment is unique to John. It is unmistakably strong.

In the same manner, the worshiper with a clear sense of calling is drawn. Then, and only then, the worshiper can lead with confidence, assurance, and focus. Nothing is as fulfilling as when the worshiper is engaging God's people in worship—personally and publicly beholding the wonder of knowing and sensing God's presence. And each time the worshiper engages in worship, God continues to rekindle, reclaim, and renew the call!

CHAPTER 3

THE CENTER

"Okay guys, you can rest your paddles. Just drink in the view," John, our guide, said with wonder in his voice.

We were about thirty minutes into our adventure on the river. We coasted quietly and gazed around the canyon as the water carried us swiftly downstream. Even the talkative Brooklyn couple sat in silent awe at the tranquility of the wilderness. We had conquered the Class I rapids, but we knew the big water was waiting for us. In these moments, John took us back to his early experiences, when he first encountered the river.

"I remember when my dad first brought me to the river. The only way to explain it is . . . it felt like home. Even as a kid, I felt the river calling me. Like it picked me. On one of my earliest trips on the whitewater, he told me some things I've never forgotten: 'You are not the center, John. The river is the center. It was here before you, and it will be here when you are gone. Remember, John, we were made for the river, not the other way around. The river does not need us, John. We need the river. Life, energy, joy, beauty, vitality, purpose—it's all in the river. Someday you will see, and then you will tell your sons and daughters.'" John craned his neck, looking around the canyon. "It's important to remember we are just a small part of the story the river is writing through this canyon."

It struck me how connected he was to this perspective, even in the company of a bunch of city-dwellers from the flatlands.

You are not the center, John. The river is the center.

Say it with me: "I am not the center. God is the center." Oh, that this truth would sink deep into our souls! This is at the very heart of the worshipful life. He is before all things and will always be. This truth must be central to how we guide people. If we for a moment make ourselves the center—our recognition, our ideas, fill in the blank—we will distort the truth and mislead those we are guiding. Becoming a great worship guide is recognizing we are not the center; he is the center. His love and power have initiated everything.

When we consider the magnificence of the galaxies, the creation of earth, the holy Scriptures, and Jesus's infinite love displayed through the cross and his infinite power displayed through the empty tomb, how could we imagine we are the center? But we so often give in to the temptation to focus on our abilities, dreams, interests, and futures. It's human nature to become myopic and self-centered. We are prone to wander. Like the Israelites, we fashion idols to bow down to. Idols of fear, self-reliance, sensuality, achievement, comfort, notoriety, approval, power, and more. We somehow think we are the central figures of history.

The river is alive and moving, carving its way through the canyons of history and bringing life, beauty, and hope. Our all-powerful, all-knowing, all-seeing, all-loving master of the universe is writing his great story. We are not the main character. Jesus is.

I am not the center. Jesus is the center of everything.

You and I are only a small part of the great story God is writing through his Son, Jesus. Jesus, and not a mere human or creature, is the principle character in God's great story. He is the focal point of all creation. All things are created by, through, and for Jesus (Rom 11:36). The universe truly does revolve around him. Look what the writer of Colossians says about the centrality of Christ:

> The Son is the image of the invisible God, the firstborn over all creation. For in him all things were created: things in heaven and on earth, visible and invisible, whether thrones or powers or rulers or authorities; all things have been created through him and for him. He is before all things, and in him all things hold together. And he is the head of the body, the church; he is the beginning and the firstborn from among the dead, so that in everything he might have the supremacy.
>
> —COLOSSIANS 1:15–18

Think about this: All of history points to Jesus. Every Old Testament message, patriarchal journey, prophetic narrative, Pentateuch guideline for worship, precious promise, and all the Psalms point to one individual: the Messiah. Jesus is the constant theme of the ages. He is the image of the invisible God. He is victor and conqueror over death. He alone has the authority to forgive sins. He alone holds the world together with his spoken word. He alone is the bright morning star. Jesus is the hope of the ages. Look at how the writer to the Hebrews addresses this subject:

> In the past God spoke to our ancestors through the prophets at many times and in various ways, but in these last days he has spoken to us

by his Son, whom he appointed heir of all things, and through whom also he made the universe. The Son is the radiance of God's glory and the exact representation of his being, sustaining all things by his powerful word. After he had provided purification for sins, he sat down at the right hand of the Majesty in heaven. So he became as much superior to the angels as the name he has inherited is superior to theirs.

—HEBREWS 1:1–4

In our earlier encounter with the river, we quickly learned that everything in the story is subservient to the river. John doesn't draw attention to himself as the river guide. He does not direct the boater's attention to his expensive gear, the sturdiness of his boat, his own unique abilities to maneuver around the most difficult river rapids, his plan for the journey, or the adventurous companions in his care. John's obsession is with the wonder, grandeur, and glory of the river. He *loves* the river. And the river is central to everything in his life!

Likewise, as worshipers, our focus cannot and must not be on ourselves. If it is, we cannot be truly said to be worshiping at all! When you and I come to Jesus and ask him to equip us as worshipers and leaders of God's people in the holy sacred rite of worship, we must comprehend and acknowledge that he is already the heart and center of all that we do.

As we internalize the truth that Jesus already reigns as our absolute, consummate, and ultimate supreme authority, we will be compelled by the Holy Spirit to enter his presence and proclaim with John the Baptist, "He must become greater; I must become less" (John 3:30). Worship is not about the experience of the worshiper. It is about Jesus.

If anything other than Jesus becomes the absolute center of our life, it will always distort our vision of who we are, including our thoughts, ambitions, goals, aspirations, and heart's desires! Jesus must be the center, the focus, the heart, the core. If he is in the center, everything else slides into place, and we will see the world and ourselves clearly.

So what is the point of all of this? We are only successful as worshipers and worship leaders when we recognize that Jesus already has preeminence (the central place) in all of life.

At some point we must all ask ourselves what is at the center of our lives. Is it our families, our music, our own worship? As we release control of our selfish, self-centered aspirations and desires, Jesus—the One that is already first in the universe—takes our feeble attempts to worship him and miraculously transforms them into humble moments of adoration that honors the one being worshiped.

CHAPTER 4

AWE AND WONDER

"Pull your paddles in guys," John said calmly, and put his finger to his lips. "Shhhh."

We coasted gently, the raft rotating ever so slowly, as if to give all of us a chance to see everything. The jagged red rock cliffs rose into the azure sky. Spruce and fir trees lined the banks as a solitary cloud passed by. Nature's sacred cathedral was breathtaking. Nothing mattered in those moments except beholding the beauty, majesty, and splendor of the river. John breathed deeply through his nose and lifted his face to the sky, his eyes closed against the radiance of the sun.

"You smell that? It's peace. It's beauty. I never tire of it. The river has been carving this canyon for thousands of years. It carries life to the valley. It sustains everything around here. Incredible, isn't it?"

"It's magnificent," Leah said under her breath.

"It's mysterious and powerful, and it never fails to show me something I haven't seen before," John continued to muse. "Inexhaustible treasures are in the river, that's what I always say."

Neal piped up, even his brashness seeming to soften. "Yep. We're a far cry from the concrete jungle back home."

"You know what is really amazing?" John asked. "The more you experience of the river, the more you want it. You will take this journey with you today, and you'll never forget it, I promise you. Just think about the sheer force of the water, the beauty of the wildlife, the power of the canyon, and that you get to experience it all. How amazing! My job is to help you see that, so that you stay amazed and come back and visit me year after year!" John was right. I've been reflecting on my experience with the river for nearly twenty years. I've not found an end to it yet.

When I consider your heavens,
　　　the work of your fingers,
　　the moon and the stars,
　　　which you have set in place,
　what is mankind that you are mindful of them,
　　　human beings that you care for them?
—PSALM 8:3–4

Wonder is the basis of worship.
—THOMAS CARLYLE

A sense of awe and wonder fueled John's continued passion and love for the river and his great sense of calling in guiding others. He was a veteran. He had run the river thousands of times, yet he was still amazed. He nurtured his ability to plumb the depths of the mystery and beauty of what he experienced daily. So much of our experience and transformation depends on our awareness. Open our eyes, Lord, that we might see!

There have been many times in my life when I have not been aware. I've missed the beauty. I was too preoccupied with my agendas, my schedule, my need to achieve. Far too often we are distracted, and our attention is arrested by social media, our own ambition, or even our ministry duties. It may not be something bad. We can be distracted by something good.

But even good things must not rob us of the wonder and amazement of who our Savior is and what he has done and is doing all around us.

> Great is the LORD and most worthy of praise;
>> his greatness no one can fathom.
> One generation commends your works to another;
>> they tell of your mighty acts.
> They speak of the glorious splendor of your majesty—
>> and I will meditate on your wonderful works.
>> —PSALM 145:3–5

The heart of the way of worship is to pay attention to the awesomeness of God. To be rapt in awe, ablaze with wonder, is to be dumbfounded, eyes wide and mouth gaping at the beauty and greatness of something that transcends our ability to fully understand or describe. Earthly wonders often teach us how to be in awe: the Swiss Alps, a break of ocean waves in Hawaii, a masterpiece of art, or an indescribable performance of music. All of these things and so much more come from the hand of the God we worship.

Our guide described the river as "mysterious and powerful" and full of inexhaustible treasures. The river isn't just full of rapids. Remember how John tells his friends to "pull the paddle in the boat" and to look and listen? Even the roughest, most tempestuous raging river will have places of calm and peace. In these moments of stillness, in the river and in our relationship to God, we can capture a sense of divine focus, direction, and purpose. Sometimes the calm water allows for a time of personal pause, a recalibration of the soul and a renewed perspective.

We experience the awe and wonder of God in the explosive and tumultuous seasons, or the magnificence of nature in a driving storm. But the Lord often speaks to our hearts during the peaceful, simple, unruffled times.

Time and time again, the Bible records God speaking to his people in the quiet. The prophet Elijah was told to listen for the still, small voice (1 Kgs 19:12).

Psalm 46:10 says, "Be still, and know that I am God." Most often, *stillness* precedes knowing. It is in the quiet that we often get a clearer picture of a magnificent God who is mysterious, beyond our ability to comprehend, yet closer than we can imagine.

John told his rafters to take time to "behold the beauty, the majesty, and the splendor of the river." Why? In beholding the beauty of God's creation, we can personally proclaim with all nature that our God is worthy of praise. Even his majesty reveals the "splendor of his wonderful works." But as important as seeing God's awe and wonder is to our understanding of God, there is more—much more!

Look again at Psalm 145:

> My mouth will speak in praise of the LORD.
>> Let every creature praise his holy name
>> for ever and ever.
>
> —PSALM 145:21

The psalmist wrote in verse 5, "They speak of the glorious splendor of your majesty—and I will meditate on your wonderful works."

Every day, no matter the circumstances, as we exalt God as king

—we enter into worship each time we meditate on his wonderful works (Ps 145:5), God opens our "spiritual eyes" and reveals something of the awe, wonder, and glory of his majesty. When we "listen for the still small voice," God opens our "spiritual ears," and we hear his words of instruction, comfort, and peace. It is most often during the quiet, tranquil moments that God "opens our minds" to apprehend and rest in "his truth." Our restful, serene moments away from the distractions of a hurried, busy world (even when we sleep; see Ps 16:7) afford opportunity for God to counsel us and impart sovereign wisdom.

God delights in drawing us, as worshipers, into his presence and providing moments of heart instruction so that we may confidently speak his name, proclaim his wonders (Ps 96:3–4), teach the next generation about his awesome power (Ps 145:3), and breathe his peace into the lives of those we guide in worship.

So how does the worshiper learn to meditate on God's wonderful works?

First, establish a special time to meet with God in worship. Jesus usually meditated in the early morning. David, the psalmist, often meditated at night (Ps 119:148). In fact, in Psalm 77:6, David calls to remembrance his song in the night. Every day, the psalmist meditates within his heart with an earnest, diligent spirit.

It doesn't really matter when we meet with God. The important thing is to find a special time to *be with, search for, extol, and meditate on* him.

Second, establish a special place to meditate on God as the Lord of wonders. Some people find solace at a beach or beside a mountain stream. Others arise early in the morning and sit at the kitchen table, coffee in hand, while reading and meditating on God. Others are drawn to a majestic canyon or mountain cliff. It really doesn't matter where. Find a place to be alone with God.

Third, establish a rhythm. In our story, John comes to this special place on the river's bend every year. John established a habit of seeing the wonder of it all—the smell, peace, rocks, trees, the water's flow.

You and I need to repeatedly practice seeing and worshiping the wonder of all that God has done and is doing in our world.

Begin by thanking God for all he is doing in this world and in your life. Acknowledge his greatness. Also, use the following, which has been adapted from Psalm 145 (NKJV), to guide your conversation of praise with the Lord. Go ahead, try it, right now:

> Great are you LORD, and greatly to be praised;
> your greatness *is* unsearchable.
> I declare your mighty acts, your greatness,
> the memory of your great goodness, and your righteousness.
> You are gracious and full of compassion,
> slow to anger and great in mercy.
> LORD, you are good to all,
> and your tender mercies *are renewed every morning.*
> All your works shall praise you, O LORD,
> and your saints shall bless you.
> They shall speak of the glory of your kingdom,
> and talk of your power,
> to make known to the sons of men your mighty acts,
> and the glorious majesty of your everlasting kingdom,
> and your dominion *endures* throughout all generations.
> —PSALM 145:3–4, 6–9, 10–13 NKJV; MODIFIED

Fourth, focus on the Lord. Meditate on his wonder, his holiness, his power, his provision, his righteousness, and his salvation. Tell him that he is lovely. Worship him. When we focus on Jesus, he will make his presence known in our lives. And in the process, he will equip us to teach and guide others to be passionate worshipers. Pray the following to the Lord:

> Oh LORD, you are righteous in all your ways,
> gracious in all your works.

Awe and Wonder

You are near to all who call upon you,

to all who call upon you in truth.

You fulfill the desire of those who fear you;

hear their cry, and save them.

You preserve all who love you.

My mouth shall continually speak (proclaim, sing, and shout)

    praise to the LORD,

My flesh and my heart shall bless your holy name forever

    and ever.

        —PSALM 145:17–21 NKJV; MODIFIED

CHAPTER 5

SPIRIT AND TRUTH

"The water is really high today, and things are going to move quickly," John said enthusiastically. "Less technical, but very fast. Make sure you pay attention. Not only for safety reasons, but for the sake of beauty."

"What makes the water particularly high right now, rain?" I asked.

"That's part of it. Mostly, our snow levels this winter were huge, and when you combine that with the onset of summer temperatures being higher than normal, the watershed snowmelt that feeds this valley is raging."

The information rolled off John's tongue effortlessly as we paddled slowly. The current was increasing little by little now, and the distant rush of whitewater, though faint, was growing louder with each stroke of our paddles.

"Wow, you know stuff," Fanny said, raising her eyebrows. "Not just a pretty face."

"Hello! I'm right here, woman!" Neal was not amused.

"Oh stop, you know I'm with you. But I call a spade a spade."

"Whatevuh."

The rest of us weren't sure if we should laugh at the awkward banter.

"I do have a masters in hydrology," John said. Maybe he wanted us to know he was more than just a hunky outdoorsman.

"Okay guys, when we round this bend, we are going to hit a great little rapid called Hank's Hoedown. There's a huge boulder in the middle of the river, and we will shoot just to the right of it. Listen closely to my commands. We don't want to get pinned. It will be fun."

The roar of the river surrounded us as we curved around the cliff. "Left forward hard!" John shouted. Our raft angled to the right. "Forward hard! All forward hard!" We shot down the rapid and grazed the giant boulder to our left. It was exhilarating. The forty-two-degree water sprayed our faces as we cheered.

"Left back hard! Right forward hard!" The raft spun quickly.

"Rest! And take a look at that." We were now floating down the river backward and looking at the postcard-like canyon we had just traversed. "Oh wow . . . so beautiful," Leah commented. The rest of the group murmured quiet agreement.

"It's not just about knowing, it's about experience too. You can't miss the beauty," John said.

"You mentioned you have a graduate degree in . . . what was it?" I asked.

"Hydrology. It's the study of the properties of water and its movement on the earth and in the atmosphere. I believe science and beauty are interwoven. If I just know the data but don't experience the beauty of the river, I might as well be in a lab somewhere. If all I did was run the river without knowledge of its nature or what's actually happening in the canyon, I miss the depth of the experience . . . the truth. Truth fuels my sense of awe and vice versa. You gotta have both if you really want to experience all the river has to offer."

John's words convinced me this was no ordinary outing. This trip was a game changer.

Yet a time is coming and has now come when the true worshipers will worship the Father in the Spirit and in truth, for they are the kind of worshipers the Father seeks. God is spirit, and his worshipers must worship in the Spirit and in truth.

—JOHN 4:23–24

Our guide said, "Truth fuels my sense of awe."

To worship God fully, we must worship him as he truly is, not a version of him that suits our liking. The more we know his character and nature, the more we respond to the revelation of who he is. His beauty, his power, and his work among us must be experienced through the lens of who he truly is as revealed in his Word. Beauty is subjective, but the properties and nature of what we call beautiful has empirical truth.

On the other hand, without emotion, depth of feeling, and experience, the truth of something can become lifeless and dead to us. If we focus solely on the "science" and never the sheer passion and emotion of being "with" the river and communing with its waters, feeling the current caress our toes, or being carried—fully immersed—in its flow, we miss the full expression, the essence.

The way of worship calls us deeper to know the truth of who God is and to enjoy and experience a surrendered communion with him. This quote from John Piper sums it up beautifully:

Truth without emotion produces dead orthodoxy and a church full of artificial admirers (like people who write generic anniversary cards for a living). On the other hand, emotion without truth produces empty frenzy and cultivates shallow people who refuse the discipline of rigorous thought. But true worship comes from people who are deeply emotional and who love deep and sound doctrine.

Strong affections for God rooted in truth are the bone and marrow of Biblical worship.

—JOHN PIPER[1]

The concept of "in spirit and truth" is foundational for those seeking to understand the way of worship. This is the underpinning and footing to everything we learn about worship in the future.

Jesus describes worshipers this way: "God is spirit, and his worshipers must worship in the Spirit and in Truth" (John 4:24).

What does this mean? And why is having these two elements—spirit and truth—*together* so important? Why not just one or the other? The words *spirit* and *truth* are strategically chosen and critically important for us to understand how we build relationship with God through our worship.

Spirit refers to our inner self, our soul. Truth refers to the revelation of God as found in his Word. In this chapter, I will focus on the all-important issue of spirit, and we will explore the idea of truth in worship in the next chapter.

What is Spirit? When there are references to "the spirit" in the Bible, this usually refers to the unseen and deepest parts of who we are—our mind, will, and emotions. This "human spirit" is the essence of what God breathed into us at creation. The very God of the universe breathed life into us. In so doing, he literally placed in Adam (the first man created) a part of himself. This is the same Spirit of God that "hovered over the face of the waters" at creation, and the same Spirit of God that spoke all of life into existence. And this is why every man, woman, boy, or girl has been *created* as a *spiritual being*, and we are alive today in our own human spirit. In reality, God is spirit, and we are not! But we are *spiritual beings* created in the image of God.

It is only natural that God created all humanity as *spiritual beings*.

In this context, the New Testament rendering for *spirit* is the word *pneuma*. So when God breathed life into man, he placed in him the breath of life, a spirit (*pneuma*). Thus, it is this *spirit* that is the essence of humanity's being. And according to the theologian and philosopher Dallas Willard, the spirit is a person's soul.[2]

This spiritual part of man, soul, is defined as the hidden or spiritual (*pneuma*) side of the person (1 Pet 3:4). Soul is the private, personal part of who we are. It is unique to each individual. Spirit in this context includes individual thoughts and feelings, along with heart or will, with its intents and choices. It also applies to an individual's bodily life and social relationships. In reality, all these things, in their inner meaning and nature, are hidden deep inside our own thoughts and feelings. And only God is the discerner of the "thoughts and attitudes" of the heart (Heb 4:12).

This hidden part of an individual provides the ability to think, love, feel, express emotion, and have an intimate relationship with God through worship. And it is this *inner self* that is transformed and redeemed when a person repents of their sin and receives the free gift of salvation through Jesus Christ.

Our *spirit* most clearly represents the image of God. As *spiritual beings*, we are created in the image of God. Solomon says in Proverbs 20:27, "The human spirit is the lamp of the Lord" It is this *spirit* that lives forever and the element within us that leaves the body when we die. Then, in the resurrection, God miraculously joins back together this very same human spirit (which has already gone to heaven after our physical body dies) with our newly resurrected bodies, and we dwell forever in the presence of the Lord Jesus Christ.

To review, when the word *spirit* and *mankind* are used together in the Bible, they refer to that immaterial part within us that actually joins together with God, who is spirit. So we are actually talking about two different spirits: the human spirit and the Holy Spirit.

How might I receive the Holy Spirit into my life?

The answer to this question is fairly simple. *Recognize that you are a sinner*, and as such, you are destined to a life without God. *Realize that only by believing in the death, burial, and resurrection of Jesus Christ* can anyone (and that includes you and me) be rescued from sin and obtain an eternal home with all the heavenly hosts. And finally, *receive Christ's presence and his Holy Spirit into your heart* (your soul or spirit or *pneuma*) as a free gift of salvation.

Once you and I receive this gift of salvation, the Holy Spirit comes to dwell or live in our being. Our *inner spirit* is unified with the Spirit of God—they become one. That is why the Bible says, "The Spirit himself testifies with our spirit that we are God's children" (Rom 8:16). And it is his Holy Spirit, *which he breathed into us at salvation*, that guides, carries, and sustains our worship of him.

So how does this impact and guide our worship of God?

First, receiving God's gift of salvation gives us focus in our worship. Worship becomes very personal, sometimes even private. When Jesus says that "God *is* Spirit, and those who worship him must worship in *spirit and truth*," he is giving us a template for loving and worshiping God.

Second, worshiping in Spirit gives us purpose. Worship *in Spirit* includes loving God with our whole being—our individual thoughts, feelings, heart, will, and intents and all the hidden things deep inside ourselves.

Third, worshiping God in Spirit gives us motive. When we worship *in Spirit*, we are immediately transformed from the inside out. Worship then includes all of our emotions, motives, intents—all of our self—in full and total surrender to God.

Finally, God is powerfully awesome and almighty—full of majesty. He is also very loving, kind and gracious. He enjoys vibrant relationship with those that worship him *in Spirit*. While God is all powerful, he is not some kind of unknown energy, universal force, or cosmic presence to be reckoned with and feared by we finite human beings.

Rather, God is a real, living, personable, immortal person that cultivates friendship with those he has created—you and me.

God, as Spirit, communicates with people of all races, creeds, ethnic origins, colors, and nationalities. Each time God guides, protects, and provides for man and woman—no matter the generation—he reveals something new and wonderful about himself. Each time he divulges something new about himself, our instinctive, unrestrained response is worship—in spirit.

In the next chapter, we will explore what it means to worship *in truth.*

CHAPTER 6

HIS WORD

The late morning sunlight warmed the canyon as it burned off the chilly fog. For a couple from the low flatlands of central Florida, it was an otherworldly experience. We had already navigated several rapids, and our group was beginning to bond over a combination of laughter and a healthy fear of the unknown.

"When are we going to do the big stuff?" Neal asked impatiently, as if he wanted to get it over with.

"Oh, it's coming. The big stuff is coming, right Anastasia?" John replied with a sinister smile, drawing the quiet Swedish apprentice into the conversation.

She smiled through her cherub-like rosy cheeks. "It vill be most exciting zis big stuff you speak of." Her thick Nordic accent and quiet manner drew us in.

"There's Mansion Rock over there. That's a great spot to camp if you are doing an overnight."

Our guide was constantly pointing out unique formations and subtle characteristics of the river and canyon.

"So how do you remember all the names of these rapids and formations?" I asked.

"When you spend as much time with the river as I do, you just remember," John said.

"How do they get their names? Did you name them?"

"Oh no, these were named for generations before I arrived. I've got them all written down in the book," John said as he patted his satchel. "My father and grandfather knew them. I heard all about it when they would tell me stories from the river."

"Wow, so this has been in the family a while," I said.

"Yeah, I'm a fourth-generation river runner."

His book intrigued me. "So is your book like a journal that you write in?"

"I definitely write thoughts in it, and draw an occasional picture, but the real gold is what was in there already."

My curiosity mounted. "So what's in there? If you don't mind me asking."

He opened up the waterproof satchel and pulled out a two-inch-thick, leather-bound book. It looked nearly antique. He untied and unwound the leather string wrapped around it and handed it to me.

"Be careful—don't drop it in the water. These are generational writings about the river from my family. It's got anecdotes, wisdom, learnings, stories. It's a treasure."

"Wow, I can't believe you bring this out on the water with you." I felt like I was holding something sacred.

"Don't worry, I've got the originals locked away. This is a copy my father made and I've kept using. It never leaves my side. It's my guidebook. I eat the words like food. It's my connection to the past and the bigger story unfolding. It's my connection to the river."

Your word is a lamp for my feet,
a light on my path.
—PSALM 119:105

For the word of God is alive and active. Sharper than any double-edged sword, it penetrates even to dividing soul and spirit, joints and marrow; it judges the thoughts and attitudes [or intents] of the heart.
—HEBREWS 4:12

It was evident that John's guidebook was a priceless treasure to him. He revered it, copied it, memorized it, and carried it with him. Describing the words like food makes it seem like he couldn't live without them. The words in that guidebook were nourishment, guidance, and light for his path. This is a beautiful picture of our desperate need for the Word of God. The Scriptures are a tangible connection to the Word, Jesus. The Bible is his love letter to his people. It is our connection to the ancient path, the story of God and his movement on the earth. It contains the wisdom of the ages, instructions for living a flourishing life, the character and nature of our Creator, and the way to relate to the Almighty. The way of worship is to know, "eat," meditate on, and obey the Word of God.

Martin Luther once said, "The soul can do without everything except the word of God, without which none at all of its wants are provided for."[1]

The Scriptures hold inexhaustible riches for everyone who will take hold of them. Forty different authors penned these sixty-six books over thousands of years to bring us an integrated, God-breathed message. These words are life. They are the very essence of who God is. To understand, experience, and live the way of worship, we must plumb the depths of these truths to commune with God. We must "taste and see" that the Lord is good. We must eat this divine food. Moment by moment, day by day we will be transformed into his image. We will discover the life we were always meant to live. This is the power of his Word.

In our last chapter study, we discussed the reality of worshiping God *in spirit*. For seekers of the way of worship, worship *in spirit* involves the expression of our love for God with all of our intents and motives, emotions, heart, and thoughts. But if we only worship God *in spirit*, our worship will become shallow and uninformed. Why? There are two essential elements to worship of God: worship involves spirit *and* truth.

Jesus said, "Yet a time is coming and has now come when the true worshipers will worship the Father *in the Spirit and in truth*, for they are the kind of worshipers the Father seeks. *God is spirit*, and his worshipers must worship in the Spirit and in truth" (John 4:23–24; emphasis added).

Truth!

What is truth? Where does one find and pursue it? Is God's truth any different than the truth all humanity endeavors to pursue?

These questions have perplexed the human mind for centuries. It all boils down to this two-fold inquiry: (1) What is truth, and (2) why does the search for truth occupy such an important and central place in the lives of people all around the world?

The word *truth* appears 217 times in 210 verses of the New King James Version (NKJV) of the Bible: 112 times in the Old Testament and 105 times in the New Testament. It is used forty times just in the Psalms, twenty-three times in John, and nineteen times in 1–3 John. It can be used as a noun, verb, or adverb.

There are three types of truth.

First, there is "truth" referring to that which is fact, reality, or absolute. Absolute truth is something that is true at all times and in all places. It is something that is always true no matter what the circumstances. It is a fact that cannot be changed.

Second, there is truth that reflects the real character of a person. It refers to the characteristics of the inner person, beyond the sight of others: truthfulness, honesty, character, integrity, or fidelity.

Third, there is truth that is found in the person of Jesus Christ. This kind of truth is also referred to as the Word of God, the Holy Spirit, and the "truth of the Gospel." This truth is totally pure, without any falsehood.

Certainly, truth is what we know to be real and right about God! Theologians often refer to this kind of truth as "God's revealed truth." But how does God reveal himself? We've already learned that God reveals himself in nature (Rom 1:20) and through life circumstances. But God also reveals truth as his Holy Spirit enlightens our mind and brings us understanding of Scripture. Our inner self, our spirit (*pneuma*), is then energized and engaged by God's truth.

The Bible gives testimony to the fact that over many centuries, God's Spirit spoke to select prophets and apostles and *breathed into them truth*—his Word. These prophets in turn penned for all of humanity God's written revelation about himself, the Bible. Why? God reveals himself to us because *he wants us to know him*. It is our responsibility to worship him from the deepest places of who we are in the truth and reality of who he is.

How do we know this truth?

First, once our spirit (pneuma) is transformed by the miracle work of salvation, his Holy Spirit dwelling within us opens our eyes to his truth! So while we should worship God with all our heart, soul, and spirit, we also need to worship God with all our mind, cognition, reasoning, understanding, and intellect—this is "knowing" God's truth.

In the words of Ronald E. Hawkins, "The joining of the Holy Spirit with the human spirit that takes place in regeneration provides the capacity for taking worship to a whole new level because the Holy Spirit prompts allegiance to the word of truth (the Scriptures) that are infused with His breath."[2] This is why Jesus could so freely claim, "I am *the way and the truth and the life*. No one comes to the Father except through me" (John 14:6; emphasis added).

God's truth is different than any other concept of truth. The Bible tells us that once we know the truth, it will make us free (John 8:32). God's truth is powerful, life changing, and eternal.

Job said, "But it is the spirit in a person, the breath of the Almighty, that gives them understanding" (Job 32:8). Again, in the words of Ronald E. Hawkins,

> Worship is the normal response of a person in whom the lamp of the human spirit has been brightened by the witness ministry of the Holy Spirit in the human Spirit. *This same Holy Spirit bears witness to the truth found in the word of God and creates a heightened desire for obedience to that truth.* The outcome of this witness is enhanced understanding of all things spiritual, the brightening of the light within the human spirit and an outflow of worship.[3]

Second, Jesus Christ is the full expression of God's truth. The Bible teaches us that "the Word became flesh and made his dwelling among us. We have seen his glory, the glory of the one and only Son, who came from the Father, full of grace and truth" (John 1:14). And Jesus told his disciples, "I am the way and the *truth* and the life. No one comes to the Father except through me" (John 14:6; emphasis added). The more we learn about Jesus, the more we understand God's truth.

Third, God's Word is truth. We worship God within the limits, safeguards, and restraints of his truth—his Word. The psalmist wrote centuries ago, "All your words are *true*; all your righteous laws are *eternal*." (Psalm 119:160; emphasis added). The Word of God is a "living document" that is powerful and life changing. In John 17:17, Jesus says that the Word of God has power to sanctify. The writer of the New Testament epistle to Hebrews reminds us,

> The word of God is alive and active. Sharper than any double-edged sword, it penetrates even to dividing soul and spirit, joints and marrow; it judges the thoughts and attitudes [or intents] of the heart.
> —HEBREWS 4:12

Fourth, God desires relationship so much that he seeks to find those that choose to worship in spirit and truth. It is God's deep desire for all the world to seek him and worship him in spirit *and truth*. Jesus said it best:

> Yet a time is coming and has now come when the true worshipers will worship the Father in the *Spirit* and in *truth*, for they are the kind of worshipers the Father seeks. God *is* spirit, and his worshipers must worship in the Spirit and in *truth*.
> —JOHN 4:23–24; EMPHASIS ADDED

According to the *Encyclopedia Britannica*, "A dedicated pursuit of truth characterizes the good scientist, the good historian, and the good detective."[4] I would add that it also characterizes the good worshiper. For the Christ-follower, the pursuit of truth is critical to understanding the power, process, and purposes of worship. So in the final analysis, what does it really mean to worship God *in spirit and truth*? And how does this apply to the way of worship?

- Worship in spirit means I give all of myself—being, soul, thoughts, intents—back to God in total surrender.

- Worship in spirit is to be joined with the Spirit of God, who lives in me after conversion, and through which my mind and intellect are awakened to God's revelation—his truth.
- Worship in truth is to recognize that all truth comes from God—all aspects of truth are involved in my worship, including facts about life, a representation of my integrity or honesty, and the truth about God.
- Worship in truth is to worship, adore, magnify, and exalt God within the boundaries of God's Word, the Bible, because God's Word is truth.

CHAPTER 7

THANKFULNESS

"We could be shopping right now," Franny said in angst.

"Are you kiddin' me?" Neal labored to turn his rotund body and look back at his wife as we paddled slowly through the canyon.

"I'm just sayin'," she said, smacking her gum.

"Do you believe this, John?" Neal looked back at our guide from the front of the raft. "She tells me she wants adventure. She tells me she wants to spend time together. I bring her half way across the country, spend a small fortune, and this is the thanks I get. She wants to go shopping!"

They didn't seem to mind that we were all witnessing their quarrel, and while it made us all a little uncomfortable, their lack of pretense was actually refreshing—in an awkward sort of way.

"What can I say, I'm an inside girl," Franny said as she shrugged.

"Can you believe the disrespect?" Neal continued, sweeping his arm to take in the canyon.

"Look around you, woman. This is unbelievable. No shopping mall could compete with this! Am I right? Huh?"

"Alright already, you big lug! I'm having fun, I'm having fun!" she replied. They grinned at each other, letting us all know it was okay to laugh.

"How's this for fun!" Neal said as he threw the blade of his paddle into the river, which sent a wave of water right at his petite wife's head.

"Oh. My. Gawd." Franny just sat there, her teased blonde hair now a wet, melted mess on her face. "You are going to pay." Everyone laughed hysterically.

A few minutes later down river, after we traversed some small Class II rapids, Franny surprised us a bit. "Okay people, I am actually grateful to be here. It wasn't my first choice but . . . I think it was the right one. I'm having fun, okay?" she said with a coy grin.

Our guide's reply is etched in my memory. "I know I'm grateful to be here. I'm grateful this is my office." He gazed at the epic scenery all around as he continued. "I'm thankful the river chose me. I'm thankful to meet new people every day, have air in my lungs, and a bright future. I think gratitude is the foundation for peace and joy, so I try to stay in that place."

We all sat silently and drank in the view.

Therefore, since we are receiving a kingdom that cannot be shaken, let us be thankful, and so worship God acceptably with reverence and awe, for our "God is a consuming fire."

—HEBREWS 12:28–29

Gratitude brings contentment, peace, joy, strength, and freedom. Gratitude makes us aware of our need. It breaks the bondage of entitlement and helps us remember where every good gift comes from. A grateful heart is an essential ingredient in the life of worship.

What made John incredibly effective as a guide was that he stayed grateful. From that place, he exuded joy, contentment, peace, and excitement for the adventure that lay ahead of us. We felt special that he was grateful for our presence. Gratitude is so contagious. It is one of the most powerful traits of any human, but especially those called to guide people to worship.

First and foremost, we are grateful to God for who he is and all he has done and continues to do. From that posture, our gratitude makes its way into our relationships, our blessings, even our storms. For God is working for our good and his glory no matter what.

Give thanks to the LORD, for he is good;
his love endures forever.
—PSALM 118:1

To those seeking to know more about the way of worship, Psalm 118:1 may be one of the most important verses in the Bible. It denotes an action—giving—and an attitude of thankfulness. These two principles are so important to God that this phrase is used at least seven more times just in the book of Psalms (Ps 107:1; 118:1, 29; 136:1–3, 26). "Give thanks!" Paul defines its scope, saying, "*Give thanks in all circumstances;* for this is God's will for you in Christ Jesus" (1 Thess 5:18; emphasis added).

In the story section of this chapter, John transforms a potential spirit of ungratefulness into a moment of praise and thanksgiving. John is captivated by the eternal wonder and calling of the river. His attitude of gratitude gives perspective and prompts him to maintain focus on the real purpose of the journey.

Gratitude is a powerful word that describes an attitude and an action. It must be both studied and cultivated as a conviction of the heart.

Every great religion, language, people group and culture develops a way of articulating gratitude, value, and appreciation. The Scriptures give "expressions of gratitude" an important theological role. Leviticus 22:29 taps into the prerequisite for gratitude by reminding worshipers, "When you offer a sacrifice of thanksgiving to the Lord, *offer it of your own free will*" (NKJV; emphasis added).

The Bible most often uses the word *thanksgiving* to express this "spirit of gratitude." In fact, thankfulness and gratitude come from the same Greek word, *eucharistia*, which means "thankfulness, gratitude, giving thanks, or thanksgiving."

"Thanksgiving" occurs forty times in the Bible (thirty-one times in the Old Testament and nine times in the New Testament). And the words *thanks, thankful,* and *thank you* appear 177 times in the English Bible. This word for gratitude, *eucharistia* or *eucharistos*, is also used to describe what God's people do around the communion table— Eucharist—a "thanksgiving celebration" of the death, burial, and resurrection of Jesus Christ.

Historically and biblically, this "gratitude attitude" is an important part of our daily walk with God. Gratitude often guides our worship. As we consider our role as leaders of worship, perhaps we should remember that thankfulness, gratitude (singing and making melody in our heart), and joy most often give evidence with a cheerful countenance or gracious disposition. Proverbs teaches us that a cheerful heart and grateful spirit are often evidence of wholesome mental, physical, spiritual, and psychological health (Prov 15:13). "A cheerful heart is good medicine" (Prov 17:22).

When maintaining an attitude of gratitude, the worshiper is able to strengthen relationships. This includes building partnerships with those around, within, and outside the worshiper's immediate sphere of influence. It supports team building, encourages collaboration, and draws in others, helping the leader bring in musicians and participants to the worshiping community. Demonstrating a spirit of grateful partnership often inspires, reassures, and even persuades those under the worshiper's care that every task in worship ministry is vitally important to the work of the ministry.

An attitude of gratitude is encouraging and edifying to the one leading worship and the worshiper alike. "Gracious words are a honeycomb, sweet to the soul and healing to the bones" (Prov 16:24). God often allows those of us leading worship an opportunity to share timely words of encouragement. These words in turn become the foundation for building up, informing, and instructing worshipers and making them into strong disciples.

Gratitude cultivates and nurtures a humble spirit. Often, the worshiper with a grateful spirit can communicate a genuine heart of thanksgiving to everyone around—the praise team, band, choir, media team, and congregation. The entire atmosphere is transformed into a worship gathering of joy. Sometimes God uses these moments of affirmation to plant and develop in the lives of the body of Christ a spirit of humility, kindness, bounty, generosity, charity, compassion, intercession, wisdom, and gladness. At the end of the day, these qualities help build character and integrity within the entire worshiping community.

The cultivation of a posture of gratitude helps develop a spirit of thanksgiving. The apostle James asks, "Is anyone happy? Let them sing songs of praise" (James 5:13). Gratitude and a thankful spirit are gifts from the Lord as his peace rules the heart and his Word dwells richly with wisdom (Col 3:15–16). As the worshiper faithfully discovers how to develop a daily walk with Christ—learning how to live the Christian graces taught in Scripture—the Holy Spirit begins to cultivate and develop a posture of gratitude that will grow into a regular habit.

How can we cultivate a heart of gratitude? The answer is simpler than you may think. We do it by remembering.

Remember to be grateful for the past, present, and future. Take time to think about all that God has given you, and consciously be thankful. Graciously honor God as Sovereign for his guidance and providence. Live a life of thanksgiving, trusting God to keep his promises and provide for your future.

Gratitude doesn't happen by accident—it is something you have to practice. *Practice demonstrating an attitude of gratitude every day.* God rewards those who develop a grateful heart. Cultivating gratitude protects you from the temptation to brood over the difficulties of a busy day or hard circumstances, because God will keep your mind occupied with himself. The joy of the Lord will become your strength, and in the process, God grants you the joy of your heart (Eccl 5:20).

Remember, gratitude is a choice. You and I, as worshipers of the most high God, have a choice between gratitude and ingratitude. An unthankful spirit kills a gratitude attitude. Ingratitude and gratitude simply cannot exist in the same spirit at the same time. Choose to be grateful. Carefully guard, protect, nurture, and practice an "attitude of gratitude."

B. HIS PURPOSES, OUR OBEDIENCE

CHAPTER 8

TIME

"I think we are going to hit the Crystals at the perfect time," John said, squinting toward the late morning sun. Our guide leaned off the back of the raft and dipped his hand in the frigid water for a few seconds before he splashed some on his face.

"What are the Crystals?" Leah asked with a touch of concern.

"You'll see in about thirty seconds." John pointed forward with one nod of his dirty-blonde hair.

We all focused our eyes downriver. The canyon opened, revealing a wide and bubbling cascade about three hundred yards long. The sun was high now, and its rays bounced off the water, sparkling like a million tiny mirrors.

"It's like the light is dancing on the water," Leah commented in awe.

"It's the river's choreography. I've always said the waters have rhythms. This proves it," John said.

My musician's mind immediately imagined assigning the sparkling reflections individual sounds and instruments. From melodic percussion to woodwinds, strings, and the like, it was all coordinated as a cohesive musical expression. A symphony of the river. It would be magical.

"You should see it in the winter!" John proclaimed.

"Oh, if the water is this cold in summah, there's no way I'd be anywhere close in winter!" Franny declared, stretching her fake-nail-bedecked finger into the air.

"It's not that bad, Franny," John replied through a sly grin. "Think Narnia."

"Think what?" she asked, perplexed.

"I thought you guys only did this in the summer months," I said.

"This is home for me, so I'm always at the river. If you are only here in the summer, you definitely get to experience the river, but there's so much more."

"I would love to see it in the fall. I bet the leaves are spectacular," Leah said.

"Totally. If you are here year-round, the river shows off in ways you just don't get otherwise. *Tourists* run the river in the summer; *river guides*, who really know the river, live here. The river speaks to me through every season. Some of the most beautiful scenes are only experienced in the harshest conditions. There are no shortcuts. It takes time . . . time with the river. There's nowhere else I'd rather be anyway."

"Sounds a little like life to me," Neal commented nonchalantly as he took a stroke with his paddle.

"Whoa, Neal waxing a little philosophical on us. I like it!" John responded.

"Hey . . . I'm deep, buddy boy. Very, very deep," Neal quipped through a smirk. We all had a good laugh.

As Jesus and his disciples were on their way, he came to a village where a woman named Martha opened her home to him. She had a sister called Mary, who sat at the Lord's feet listening to what he said. But Martha was distracted by all the preparations that had to be made. She came to him and asked, "Lord, don't you care that my sister has left me to do the work by myself? Tell her to help me!"

"Martha, Martha," the Lord answered, "you are worried and upset about many things, but few things are needed—or indeed only one. Mary has chosen what is better, and it will not be taken away from her."

—LUKE 10:38–42

"It takes time . . . time with the river." John's statement rings in my memory. Is there any more valuable commodity that we possess than time? Everything in our culture fights for it. If we are not excruciatingly intentional, we will give our time to things that do not matter. It is a limited resource. Once time is spent, it can never be recovered.

Jesus's words, "Mary has chosen what is better and it will not be taken away from her," give us his explicit thoughts on what he desires and what is best for us. His response to Martha's frustration with her sister's lack of attentiveness to the chores at hand says our attention *to* him is more important than our activity *for* him. Let that sink in. Private devotion is more desired by our Savior than public service.

It was evident that our guide dedicated time to the river. His awe and love for the river—his knowledge of it and its movement on the earth, his ability to guide us over it and point out all the beautiful things about it—flowed from the well of time he had invested. He knew the waters through every season because he spent the time.

When they saw the courage of Peter and John and realized that they were unschooled, ordinary men, they were astonished and they took note that these men had been with Jesus.

—ACTS 4:13

When Peter and John were brought before the rulers and religious leaders to give an account for the miraculous impact their ministry was having, their courage and spiritual authority caused all to "take note that these men had been with Jesus."

The way of worship calls us into a life that makes it clear that we too have been with Jesus. Oh that we would be drenched in the waters of his power and presence. We must sit at his feet, hanging on his every word. We must spend time with him. He is the only One who has healing, guidance, mercy, and love waiting for us, if only we have the time.

As we continue on our journey on the way of worship, we come to one of the most important issues facing us during these busy days: time with Jesus! Isn't it curious that our God—who is not bound by time, space, or the constraints of our definition of time—desires for those he created to spend time in his presence? God delights in spending time with you and me.

Why? It takes time to build relationship with another person—it's a process. It's no different when establishing a dynamic, vibrant, warm relationship with Jesus. There is no substitute for time. The depth of any relationship with Jesus is largely going to be correlated to the amount of personal, one-on-one time together—knowing, seeking, discovering, and understanding more about Jesus. It is crucial to our spiritual journey that we surrender all of our time to Jesus. In fact, perhaps the most important time to guard, love, protect, understand, and nurture are the moments spent with Jesus.

Time is a wonderful, personal gift from God. Each person is given the same number of hours in a day to steward. We all have opportunity to guard, protect, develop, and be held accountable for the time God has allotted in any given day. Time is freely received and spent by each person according to their own ability to be intentional and disciplined. Time doesn't cost anything. Yet it is priceless. It's a free gift from God. But time is also one of the most precious and expensive commodities and treasures owned by every human on the planet. Why? Time is a life-long experience that we are all required to diligently steward.

The word *time* is used to indicate a duration, occasion, age, season, tempo, rhythm, moment, or lifetime. It can refer to a plan or schedule, or even to when something should happen or be done, like a deadline. In creating or performing a musical composition, "time" indicates the rhythm or beat.

The concept is important to the Lord too. In fact, the word *time* is mentioned at least 710 times in the NKJV translation of the Bible—518 times in the Old Testament, 192 times in the New Testament. The term is referred to sixty-four times in the wisdom books, eighty-five times in the Gospels, thirty-four times in Acts, sixty-four times in the Epistles, and no less than ten times in Revelation. You get the idea. God places great emphasis on how we understand time.

The Old Testament preacher uses time to frame his commentary on life. He provides a bird's-eye view of life and reminds us all that our experience and existence on this earth is measured by moments and seconds:

> There is a time for everything,
>> and a season for every activity under the heavens:
>
>> a time to be born and a time to die,
>> a time to plant and a time to uproot,
>> a time to kill and a time to heal,
>> a time to tear down and a time to build,
>> a time to weep and a time to laugh,
>> a time to mourn and a time to dance,
>> a time to scatter stones and a time to gather them,

a time to embrace and a time to refrain from embracing,

a time to search and a time to give up,

a time to keep and a time to throw away,

a time to tear and a time to mend,

a time to be silent and a time to speak,

a time to love and a time to hate,

a time for war and a time for peace.

—ECCLESIASTES 3:1–8

The preacher continues his commentary by reminding us that God makes "everything beautiful in [his] time. He has also set eternity [infinite or unending time] in the human heart" (Eccl 3:11).

The psalmist uses the word *time* as a noun to describe a "season of trouble" or even moments for praise and worship:

The Lord is a refuge for the oppressed,

a stronghold in times of trouble.

—PSALM 9:9

For in the time of trouble

He shall hide me in His pavilion;

In the secret place of His tabernacle

He shall hide me;

He shall set me high upon a rock.

—PSALM 27:5 NKJV

I will extol the LORD at all times;

his praise will always be on my lips.

—PSALM 34:1

He is their stronghold in time of trouble.

—PSALM 37:39

Time is divided into three aspects: past, present, and future. The study of the past is history.[1] The present is what you are experiencing at any given moment.[2] And, of course, the future has not arrived yet. There is a type of study of the future called futurology,[3] but we all try to predict the future to one degree or another, through our plans and purposes.

For those seeking to know more about the way of worship, so much of the relationship with God centers around time. The writer of Romans reminds us that "God demonstrates his own love for us in this: While we were still sinners, Christ died for us" (Rom 5:8). And at just the right time in history, the apostle writes,

God sent his Son, born of a woman, born under the law, to redeem those under the law, that we might receive adoption to sonship.
—GALATIANS 4:4–5

God wants us to steward all of our time—the past, the present, and the future—for his good pleasure. The great worship leader and songwriter Frances Havergal articulates this kind of surrender by saying:

Take my life, and let it be
Consecrated, Lord, to Thee;
Take my moments and my days,
Let them flow in ceaseless praise,
Let them flow in ceaseless praise.[4]

There are several ways to accomplish this.

First, set aside a special time to be with Jesus. This principle is first introduced in chapter 4. It is reintroduced here to place even greater emphasis on the fact that our Lord desires time with you and me. Jesus taught his disciples to *prioritize their schedules* and spend time alone with him. In Mark 6:31-32, Jesus says to his disciples, "Come *with* *me by yourselves* to a *quiet place,*" and they went off by themselves "to *a solitary place*" (Mark 6:31–32; emphasis added). God wants us to be good stewards of the moments we spend with him. (More about this stewardship principle below.)

Set aside a specific time and go to a designated place where you can get away from all the distractions and busyness of the self-centered culture we live in today. In this solitary place, you can take time to build an intimate, warm, personal relationship with Jesus. That is what Jesus desires: a special time where only you and Jesus can communicate one-on-one. This is a place where you totally focus on Jesus and his Word to you. The "set time" of day doesn't really matter. I choose to spend my time with the Lord first thing in the mornings. Others choose to spend moments with God during their noontime meal or at the close of day. What matters is that you set aside "a special time and place" to be with Jesus.

Second, spend time alone with Jesus. Often we set aside time to be with Jesus, but we occupy these precious moments with other things. We get distracted by the urgency of getting tasks accomplished, organizing our day, or setting up our to-do list. But God yearns for intimacy with the very person he has created. It's not enough to just set aside a time and place to be with Jesus. One needs to actually follow through and *spend time alone with Jesus.* Jesus desires to have *alone time* with you and me. In the words of David Wilkerson, "There will come a tug from the Lord and he will whisper, 'Come alone—shut the door—let it be just the two of us.'"[5] Jesus told his disciples, "When you pray, go into your room, close the door and pray to your Father, who is unseen. Then your Father, who sees what is done in secret, will reward you." (Matt 6:6).

The way of worship calls us into time *alone with Jesus* because he loves you! As Wilkerson says, "Secret, closet prayer is the most intimate thing you can share with your Lord."[6] If you and I don't spend time alone with Jesus, we will never get to know him, love him, enjoy him, or fully trust him. Building this kind of relationship takes time away from our everyday worries and distractions. William M. Runyan, the author of the famous song "Great Is Thy Faithfulness," captures the sense of this "alone time with Jesus" task in this song written in 1923:

> *Lord, I have shut the door,*
> *Speak now the word*
> *Which in the din and throng*
> *Could not be heard;*
> *Hushed now my inner heart,*
> *Whisper Thy will,*
> *While I have come apart,*
> *While all is still.*
> *In this blest quietness*
> *Clamorings cease;*
> *Here in Thy presence dwells*
> *Infinite peace;*
> *Yonder, the strife and cry,*
> *Yonder, the sin:*
> *Lord, I have shut the door,*
> *Thou art within!*[7]

In the words of Oswald Chambers, "Jesus says to 'shut your door.' Having a secret stillness before God means deliberately shutting the door on our emotions and remembering Him. God is in secret and He sees us from the secret place. He does not see us as other people do."[8]

Third, steward your time with Jesus. You and I have the responsibility to steward our time with Jesus well. We are tasked with the responsibility to manage, preside over, supervise, and regulate the amount of time to do the tasks God places in our heart of hearts. While we need to remember that time is an event or maybe even a season, it is also a commodity that we must treasure, nurture, and guard with all diligence. Setting parameters to make sure your time with Jesus is full of rest, learning, development, and growth may help you steward that time better.

Fourth, we must redeem the time—seize the moment! On two occasions in the Bible, we are instructed to "redeem the time." In Ephesians 5:16, the rationale for redeeming (or buying up) the time is associated with the identification of an evil culture. Colossians 4:5 instructs Christians to "be wise in the way you act toward outsiders; make the most of every opportunity." This literally means "to make a wise and sacred use of every opportunity for doing good . . . make the time our own."[9] The idea here is that we should seize every moment as God's moment and steward those minutes and seconds for the glory of God and testimony of Jesus Christ.

What are the results or benefits of spending time with Jesus as a way of worship? People spending time with Jesus are transformed! They are forever changed!

The metaphor above references Acts 4:13, which demonstrates how spending time with Jesus transforms Peter and John. Those around these two disciples take note and quickly realize where their unique, personal, deeply spiritual qualities came from: "When they saw the courage of Peter and John and realized that they were unschooled, ordinary men, they were astonished and *they took note that these men had been with Jesus*" (emphasis added).

People quickly recognize a person who has spent genuine, holy time with Jesus. The New Testament disciples of Jesus recognized that they were spending time with someone special. They set aside *years* to follow and learn from Jesus, resulting in lives transformed by the working of the Holy Spirit.

We too must set aside time to learn to love Jesus for who he is and for all he has done through his eternal sacrifice. We must take time to look to Jesus as the author and finisher of our faith. We must take time to listen to Jesus, understand his words, and fully enjoy the wonder of his presence. We must take time to learn from Jesus and to sit at his feet in total surrender to his purposes and plan for our lives. We must take time to receive help from Jesus.

If you and I will "swing the door of [our lives] fully open and pray to [our] Father who is in the secret place, every public thing [in our lives] will be marked with the lasting imprint of the presence of God."[10]

CHAPTER 9

CHARACTER

"Left forward," John said.

With just a few strokes from our team on the left, the raft pointed starboard, toward the bank.

"Forward hard," our guide said more forcefully. "Let's get across this current. I've got something I want to show you, and we'll take a little breather."

John never missed an opportunity to magnify the nuances and uncommon traits of the river. His contagious and intimate knowledge ignited my own desire to learn more.

Our raft slid onto the beach. I could feel the smooth stones of the bank under the canvas bottom.

Neal and I jumped out and pulled the raft farther up. The rest splashed in the shallow water and plodded ashore.

"This is a great little spot for a break before we hit some bigger goodies." John's eyebrows raised as he grinned.

"I need a sandwich." Neal rifled through his drybag. He lumbered over and lowered himself down on a felled tree that rested on a rock.

When his weight settled on part of the tree that was off the ground, it snapped, dropping the New Yorker with a thud onto the sand.

"Need is not the right word," Franny said with a sly laugh.

"What the . . . ?! Why you bustin' on me woman?" Neal quipped.

"You okay, man?" I asked, though I couldn't help chuckling.

"Yeah, I'm fine. That tree don't look so good though."

Franny began to dust the sand off his backside.

"Hey, hey—there's people here!" Neal exclaimed.

Everyone was laughing.

"You guys are incredible," John said, redirecting the conversation. "My grandpa used to say, 'What you see isn't always what you get.' That tree looked good on the outside, but the inside told a different story. You apply some pressure, and because of the rot, it lets you down."

"That sounds like a people lesson too," I commented.

"Exactly." John got more intense as he pulled a cooler out of the raft. "Character is all. While you have to take care of your body to run the river, what is inside—your core, your values—is everything. My grandpa also said, 'If you don't stand for something, you'll fall for anything.' If you don't have character, you don't have anything."

"It sounds like your grandpa was an amazing man," I said.

"Nope, he was a wretched drunk, a liar, and a thief." It got really quiet for several seconds, then John grinned. "Just kidding!"

Our group broke out into relieved laughter.

For this very reason, make every effort to add to your faith goodness; and to goodness, knowledge; and to knowledge, self-control; and to self-control, perseverance; and to perseverance, godliness; and to godliness, mutual affection; and to mutual affection, love. For if you possess these qualities in increasing measure, they will keep you

from being ineffective and unproductive in your knowledge of our
Lord Jesus Christ.

—2 PETER 1:5–8

Character is who you are at your very core. It is what you and I are
when no one else is around. It is "the aggregate of features and traits
that form the individual nature of some person or thing."[1]

The traits that define us, the choices we make, and the guiding
values that govern our thoughts and actions play a huge roll in our
effectiveness in life generally and as guides specifically. But it is very
tempting to chase a reputation instead, trying to control what others
think about us rather than intentionally forging the thing that matters most: character.

As Abraham Lincoln is purported to have said, "Nearly all men
can stand adversity, but if you want to test a man's character, give him
power." In our story, John said, "You apply some pressure, and because
of the rot, it lets you down." This insightful comment applies to being
a follower of Jesus, a worshiper, a good husband, wife, son or daughter,
friend and even more, someone who is called to lead others. If we do
not intentionally build and care for the strength of our character, the
rot of sin will have its way via selfishness, pride, envy, and the like,
leading to a great fall. The destruction poor character can bring will
not stop at just letting someone down or disappointing someone. It
can destroy relationships, set fire to ministries, and ultimately lead
people astray.

If "character is all," as John said, how do we build it, fortify it, and
protect it?

I'm reminded of the story of Nehemiah.

When our enemies heard that we were aware of their plot and
that God had frustrated it, we all returned to the wall, each to our
own work.

From that day on, half of my men did the work, while the other half were equipped with spears, shields, bows and armor. The officers posted themselves behind all the people of Judah who were building the wall. Those who carried materials did their work with one hand and held a weapon in the other.

—NEHEMIAH 4:15–17

They worked with one hand to rebuild the wall, while the other hand held a weapon to defend it. To fortify our character means we must take an intentional look at the virtues of godly character in Scripture and apply them to our lives by the power of the Holy Spirit. Every decision, the position of our hearts, and every nuance of our leadership must be guided by that sense of character as gleaned from God's Word.

The way of worship encompasses and cultivates a commitment to personal character. As we have seen in our last three lessons, worship begins with a heart of surrender. And character begins in the heart.

The story from Nehemiah helps us examine more closely how worship and character are related. Nehemiah, Ezra, and the Judaeans returning to Jerusalem committed themselves to rebuilding the wall around the great city of God. Their enemies—the Samaritans, Ammonites, Arabs, and Philistines—sought to destroy, defeat, distract, and discourage the Judaeans at every turn. But what the Judaeans lacked in skill, equipment, and personnel as warriors, they made up for in character. God honored Nehemiah and Ezra's commitment to doing right and enabled them to complete the wall in a mere fifty-two days (Neh 6:15–16).

Nehemiah was insightful, wise, prayerful (Neh 4:4–5), pure in faith, deep in character, powerfully courageous, and consistent in allowing the joy of the Lord to be his strength (Neh 4:11–20; 8:10). He led the people from despair in the midst of rubble (Neh 4:10) to delight and rejoicing—so much so that "the sound of rejoicing in Jerusalem could be heard far away" (Neh 12:43).

Godly character is an essential quality for those seeking the way of worship. Historically, the word *character* has been understood as "the sum qualities that define a person."[2] The famous poet and author Ralph Waldo Emerson said that "men of character are the conscience of the society to which they belong."[3]

You cannot buy character, and you cannot earn it. No one can claim to own someone else's character. It is highly personal, and it must be cultivated. Sometimes the only quality a person can bring to a gathering is their character—their honesty, the discernment between right and wrong, and the determination to *always* do *right*, especially when no one is watching.

In worship, character involves being everything one claims to be. Having good character means you are honest, truthful, honorable, and upright. Character in worship is critical to faithful communication with God.

In the metaphor above, we asked how we can build, fortify, and protect our character. I believe this is accomplished through a life of worship, primarily in four ways.

First, worship engages the process for "building" character. Character is most often demonstrated by life actions, but the true test of character resides in the heart.[4] While there are many reasons for doing good and upholding morality, true and godly character is compelled by right action and right motive: love and worship of Jesus. Honest, holy character is based on a heart committed to glorifying and pleasing God in all things (1 Thess 4:1; Col 3:23–24).

Christian character is an outgrowth and product of the Holy Spirit's work in the heart of every worshiper. Character begins in the heart and represents everything a person is *inside*. That is why the Bible tells us to guard and protect our hearts with all diligence: "Above all else, guard your heart, for everything you do flows from it" (Prov 4:23).

This proverb describes that which comes bubbling up from out of the heart. How we react to life circumstances and what we do when no one is watching is the "wellspring" (WEB), or source, of our actions. It reveals our true motives and desires. When we demonstrate unholy character, it's because those thoughts and actions have been nurtured in our heart first—they are bubbling up from within. Likewise, when we demonstrate godly character, it is an indication the Holy Spirit has done a work in our hearts, and we are seeking righteousness.

When the Holy Spirit renovates a person from the inside out, that person's character is changed. The Holy Spirit transforms a self-centered, narcissistic, unbelieving, prideful heart into a warm, passionate Christ-worshiper committed to developing and displaying character marked by the fruits of the Spirit—love, joy, peace, forbearance, kindness, goodness, faithfulness, gentleness, and self-control (Gal 5:22–23).

Worship then becomes the wellspring for developing spiritual character. The Holy Spirit emerges as the foundational source of true Christian character. Jack Hayford explains, "Character, according to Romans 5:4, produces hope. But character also seeks to cultivate the kind of disciplined life that bears the fruit of the Holy Spirit."[5]

Second, worship energizes and empowers us to "fortify" godly character. Helen Keller once said, "Character cannot be developed in ease and quiet. Only through experience of trial and suffering can the soul be strengthened, vision cleared, ambition inspired, and success achieved."[6] Character building is an ongoing, active, lifelong process. God most often uses difficult circumstances to refine, perfect, enhance, and cultivate Christian character. That's because the true test of a person's Christian character emanates, extends, and grows through times of challenging circumstances.

It is often in the most grueling and strenuous circumstances that worship brings us into a stronger relationship with our holy God, making us more and more like him. And the circumstances—no matter how arduous the testing—produce in us a character like that of

God himself. So that "afterwards we can see the result, a quiet growth in grace and character" (Heb 12:11 TLB).

Third, worship endows and supplies insight to "protect" our character. God deeply cares about our character. Some Bible scholars even refer to the Bible as a "character textbook."[7] That's because much of the Bible is filled with instructions, guidelines, and principles on how to live righteously. When we spend time worshiping Jesus—loving, adoring, seeking, and honoring him and learning at his feet—our character is nurtured and strengthened. In so doing, God turns our heart away from ungodly character—uncleanness, evil desires, covetousness, disobedience, anger, wrath, malice, filthy language, lying, and stealing. God begins to transform our hearts and develop godly character and ethical accountability—moral integrity, courage, honesty, compassion, tender mercies, kindness, humility, meekness, longsuffering, the peace of God, and self-discipline (see Col 3:5–15). He even replaces the temptation to be prideful and self-serving with a deep desire for humility and servant leadership.

Fourth, worship establishes patterns and strategies for developing spiritual character. God uses our time in worship to develop a heart for holiness and nurture our motives. W. S. Bruce suggests that the transformed character traits from Colossians 3:12–15 "go into the shaping and coloring of a man's character."

During our times of intimate, personal fellowship with the Lord, the Holy Spirit takes the opportunity to develop a profound and "ultimate habit of will" that is consistently shaped by the awakening of the Word of God in our lives. And "as we are faced with varying circumstances each day and judge and decide how to act, *our actions become our habits and our habits become our character*."[8] It is this deeply personal and transformational work of the Holy Spirit that shapes and develops character.

Why? God is calling and looking for worshipers who are authentic. The type of character you have is a choice. One writer says that "your character is the sum total of your life choices."[9] We may not have opportunity to choose the circumstances and situations we're facing, but we always have a choice in the way we respond. The sixteenth president of the United States, Abraham Lincoln, said, "Character is like a tree and reputation like a shadow. The shadow is what we think of it; the tree is the real thing."[10]

Why is this critical to the worship leader? Character represents a person's honesty before the Lord *and* people. The apostle Paul says, "Whatever you do, work at it with all your heart, as working for the Lord, not for human masters. . . . It is the Lord Christ you are serving" (Col 3:23–24). Commitment to character represents our own personal confidence in El Shaddai, our belief that God is faithful to his own Word, and our commitment to worship YHWH alone.

The story is told of Franz Joseph Haydn (1732–1809) attending a concert at the Vienna Music Hall, where his oratorio *The Creation* was being performed. Weakened by age and sickness, the great composer was confined to a wheelchair. As the majestic work moved along, the audience was caught up with tremendous emotion. When the passage "And there was light!" was reached, the chorus and the orchestra burst forth in such power that the crowd could no longer restrain its enthusiasm. They stood and cheered in thunderous, spontaneous applause.

Haydn struggled to stand. He motioned for silence. With eyes raised toward heaven and a hand pointed toward the clouds, he said, "No, no, not from me, but from thence comes all!"[11] The great composer understood something that the apostle Paul had learned centuries before: *Only God is worthy to receive glory, honor, and praise.* The character of a God-centered heart will naturally give God *all* the credit. Even in the composition of a great symphony—especially about the creation of all life—God is the source of all creativity. Haydn's character was demonstrated best when he refused to take credit for something only God can do.

A man's best collateral is his character.[12]

CHAPTER 10

FRESH ENCOUNTERS

"Neal, have you recovered okay?" John asked as he stood at the mouth of a path leading into the forest.

"Good to go, boss!"

"Okay everyone, keep your PFDs with you, and follow me."

It took me a second to remember what that stood for. Anastasia held up her personal flotation device, knowing some of us wouldn't remember. We called them life vests growing up.

"Are there snakes in here? There bettah not be snakes!" Franny yelled.

John turned and walked backward, facing us. "Probably not. I can't guarantee no snakes; this is, after all, the wild. Definitely watch out for bears, though."

Franny stopped, folded her arms, and stomped her foot. "Am I laughing? No, I am not laughing! I'm not going in there!"

John cupped his hands and called back to her, "Your chances of getting eaten are much higher if you're by yourself. You might want to stay with us!"

He turned back around and kept moving.

"Ugh!" she muttered as she hurried to keep up.

Anastasia waited for Franny with a kind smile and walked beside her as we made our way into the forest.

The canopy of fir and juniper trees shaded the well-worn clay path. The dewy air was fresh, and the fragrant scent of the woods reminded me of Christmas. The terrain began to rise sharply as we hiked deeper in. After about fifteen minutes of steady climbing, John stopped at a sharp turn in the path.

As we all caught up, Neal panted heavily and bent over, putting his hands on his knees.

"You okay, bud?" John asked as he put his hand on his shoulder.

Out of breath, Neal still managed to joke. "Fat boy tired. Fat boy tired," he gasped.

"Take your time, man."

After a few seconds, Neal signaled he was ready.

"We are coming up on The Towers," John said. "You guys are going to love this."

We continued around the bend in the path, and the dense tree line opened like a theater stage curtain to reveal a masterpiece view. We stood atop a large monolith protruding out into the canyon.

"Check it out!" John exclaimed.

We were in awe. Now, at least five stories above the river, we took in the magnificent vista. A hawk perched high in a spruce on the opposite red rock cliff, watching over the scene. The water flowed gently, deep, and wide below.

I put my toes on the edge of the cliff and peered over.

Leah grabbed the back of my shirt. "Uh, please get back, mister."

"How deep is that water?" I asked John.

"Deep enough to jump in!" John said gleefully.

"Come on, we'll go together!" I looked at Leah.

She peered over the steady swirl below.

"There's all kinds of ways to encounter the river. It's never the same. You've gotta be all in. Just jump and let the current take you back down to where we put the raft out," John said.

After we both got the courage up, we grabbed hands and leapt off the rocky ledge. The cold water took our breath away as we plunged in. It carried us gently downstream. Immediately, our experience with the river went deeper, literally and figuratively. The fear lessened. We were connected in a fresh way.

> Whom have I in heaven but you?
> And earth has nothing I desire besides you.
> My flesh and my heart may fail,
> but God is the strength of my heart
> and my portion forever. . . .
> But as for me, it is good to be near God.
> I have made the Sovereign LORD my refuge;
> I will tell of all your deeds.
> —PSALM 73:25–26, 28

One of the most moving attributes of the nature of God is that he desires relationship with us. He knows the deepest hopes and longings of our souls will only be fulfilled in a living, breathing, surrendered relationship with him. The psalmist says, "But as for me, it is good to be near God." He knows that the source of all rest, strength, peace, joy, victory, and salvation comes from the Lord.

> Deep calls to deep
> in the roar of your waterfalls;
> all your waves and breakers
> have swept over me.

By day the Lord directs his love,

at night his song is with me—

a prayer to the God of my life.

—PSALM 42:7–8

Any rich and intimate relationship requires fresh encounters: new experiences together, new conversations, and a continued journey toward each other. As life goes on, we change and morph, and there is always something new to be discovered. Leah and I have been married now for more than twenty-five years, and we are daily learning about each other. Life has its routines of work, taking care of our children and home, and the like. We are truly blessed in those things. How we treasure one another, however, is the bedrock of a healthy home. If all we did was pay bills, talk about schedules, and give each other lists of things to do, our relationship would become transactional and work-related. But there's so much more.

How much more important that we allow for and pursue fresh encounters with the Most High. All my life, I've heard the leadership axiom, "You cannot take people somewhere you've never been."

It was evident to all of us that John knew where to stop, the path to climb, and the jump to make so we could have a fresh encounter with the river. May we spend the time to encounter the river of life afresh for ourselves so that we may faithfully guide others to take the plunge.

Fresh encounters with God are part of the way of worship. The relationship God has with us is dynamic, ever-changing, energetic, fresh, vibrant, and meaningful. Each time we enter into intimate fellowship with God, he reveals something special, new, and awesome about himself to us. Our response? Worship. The more we worship him in spirit (with our total being) and truth (with our total understanding of who he is), the more God develops and enlarges, nurtures and cultivates our relationship with him.

Our worship of God, in its simplest form, is both formational and transformational. It is formational because time alone with God shapes us—our character, thoughts, integrity, person, and our total being. It is transformational because time alone with God changes us—our thinking, disposition, heart attitude, pride or arrogance, and inclination to sin. We are changed into the image of God's son, Jesus! Old things pass away. We are new and fresh from the inside out. But worship is also relational. Jesus died and lives today—victorious over death and the grave—so that you and I can have a dynamic, growing, meaningful relationship with God. We come to God as flawed, sinful, carnal, and self-serving humans through Jesus Christ and his blood atonement on the cross. We are in need of a Savior. Jesus more than qualifies to present us to God as transformed servants—humble, free from pride, eager to serve, and hungry to know more about the relationship we can have through worship.

Why is a fresh encounter a way of worship? A new experience with God is critical for those seeking to know and understand the way of worship because it renews our spirit, refocuses our insight toward that which is good and pure, revives our purposes for living, and reengages our search for truth. The Bible acknowledges that our relationship with God does not rest on a one-and-done experience, saying his mercies are "new every morning" (Lam 3:22–23).

What Does It Mean to Have a Fresh Encounter?

When our worship leads us to experience a fresh encounter with God, we enjoy a deeper, more personal relationship. We are able to *understand* the awesomeness of God's character, *view* more clearly how our plans line up with his purpose for our lives, *submit* ourselves to the working of the Holy Spirit in our heart, and better *nurture* this relationship through honest, heart-felt love (worship) of our Lord. This fresh encounter provides the fuel we need to meet the challenges of a new day.

How does one have a fresh encounter? Three very basic ingredients provide a basis for us to establish a regular, fresh encounter with God

One way is to establish a special place to meet with God, as we discussed in the two previous chapters. Down through the ages, encounters with God are almost always at some special place or location. This is partly so that the encounter can be remembered and the location revisited. Abraham, Moses, Jacob, and Joshua built altars for worship at the place of encounter. Jesus chose to go up and into the mountains for regular meetings with God. Other encounters with God are on a boat, in a house, on a highway, in a sycamore tree, and in the sanctuary.

Another way is to establish a specific *time* to meet with God, as we talked about in chapters four and eight. The issue here has more to do with the frequency of our time with God than the exact time or location. The psalmist writes, "The whole earth is filled with awe at your wonders; *where morning dawns, where evening fades, you call forth songs of joy*" (Ps 65:8; emphasis added). Here the psalmist declares that worship is given when the morning dawns and again when evening fades. Set a time and determine to meet God at a special place and you will soon experience a fresh encounter.

But the most important way to keep your relationship fresh is to experience the goodness of God firsthand. The Bible gives us the invitation to "*taste and see* that the LORD *is* good; blessed *is* the one *who* takes refuge in him!" (Ps 34:8; emphasis added).

Now, it's time to practice worshiping. Psalm 96 provides a practical, five-fold outline for experiencing God's goodness through worship— the kind of worship that opens the door for a fresh encounter.

1. Practice Singing to the Lord a New Song (vv. 1–2)

The emphasis is on singing to the Lord and not just about him. Remember, you are engaging a relationship. God wants you to sing directly to him. He wants to enjoy your song. The new song is not as much about a newly written composition but about singing from a fresh, new encounter with God.

Instructions are given to praise and proclaim his name. Proverbs 18:10 declares that "the name of the LORD is a fortified tower; the righteous run to it and are safe." Psalm 7:17 encourages us to "give thanks to the LORD because of his righteousness" and "sing the praises of the name of the LORD Most High." And Psalm 18:49 instructs us to give thanks among the gentiles and sing praises to the name of the Lord. Our praise is first to God and then proclaimed to all people everywhere. The heartbeat of this instruction is to bless, brag about, exalt, and magnify his name.

2. Proclaim His Wonders among the Heathen (vv. 3–6)

Proclaiming his wonders, marvelous works, and deeds is meticulously tied to relational worship of Jehovah. The instruction includes proclaiming his wonders to all people. Your personal testimony of God is an important part of this. God wants all people to know of the wondrous work he is doing in your life. Now is the time to tell it.

3. Give to the Lord (vv. 7–8)

Most often, we come to this principle and we think of giving money. While financial generosity is important, God doesn't need our money. The most important thing is how we give: he does want us to give of our substance out of a grateful heart and willing spirit (2 Cor 9:6–8), not grudgingly or of necessity. And we have much more than just money to give to the Lord of glory. Give him all the credit for the things he is doing in our midst. Give him our strength. Give him praise and thanksgiving. Give him your time and energy. That is how we become an offering to the Lord.

4. Enter His Presence through Prayer (v. 9)

This is where our fresh encounter will be the most obvious. Here, in his presence, we are to bring him glory and tremble before him, showing our respect. The instruction is to enter his presence boldly, reverently, regularly, and righteously as redeemed children—and with full confidence that God will intercede on our behalf. Oswald Chambers describes this kind of worship encounter:

> Think of prayer as the breath in our lungs and the blood from our hearts. Our blood flows and our breathing continues "without ceasing"; we are not even conscious of it, but it never stops. And we are not always conscious of Jesus keeping us in perfect oneness with God, but if we are obeying Him, He always is. Prayer is not an exercise, it is the life of the saint. Beware of anything that stops the offering up of prayer. "Pray without ceasing . . . "—maintain the childlike habit of offering up prayer in your heart to God all the time.[1]

5. Feed on His Word (vv. 10–13)

This part of our encounter with God engages the mind and the heart. When we encounter God, we are compelled to spend *time* in the Word, *listen* to the sweet voice of the Holy Spirit, *see* the work of God in all creation, and *rejoice* in his truth. This is critical to our fresh encounter because time in the Word feeds the soul, renews the mind, and energizes the spirit. Listening to the sweet voice of the Holy Spirit provides instruction for growth and encouragement for service. Seeing the work of God in creation confirms our faith, cancels doubt, and calls us to worship. Rejoicing in his truth helps us get our priorities straight, set God's plan in our heart, and surrender to God's purposes.

So how do we respond to a fresh encounter as we learn to practice the way of worship? Psalm 100 provides a practical recipe for expressing praise to our God: *shout* to the Lord, *serve* the Lord, and *sing* to the

Lord—a song of thanksgiving (v. 4); a song of praise (v. 4); a song of truth (v. 4); and a song of goodness (v. 5).

> Make a joyful shout to the LORD, all you lands!
> Serve the LORD with gladness;
> Come before His presence with singing.
> Know that the LORD, He is God;
> It is He who has made us, and not we ourselves;
> We are His people and the sheep of His pasture.
> Enter into His gates with thanksgiving,
> And into His courts with praise.
> Be thankful to Him, and bless His name.
> For the LORD is good;
> His mercy is everlasting,
> And His truth endures to all generations.
> —PSALM 100 NKJV

CHAPTER 11

BROKENNESS

"Okay guys, Hitchen's Twins is coming. She's a tough little rapid. Very technical and a little fussy. If you don't treat her right, she will likely flip you. I don't like to flip, so everybody please listen up." At John's husky commands, we perked up our ears.

"You sure this rapid isn't named Franny?" Neal nodded and grinned.

"Oh man. That's pretty icy, dude," I commented.

All eyes darted to Franny to capture what hoped to be an epic reaction her glare quickly turned to a smile.

"Oh, she knows! She knows!" Neal guffawed.

We followed John's commands flawlessly as our raft darted between two fallen boulders, then bucked up and down like a wooden rollercoaster through the churning whitewater. The waves of water cascaded over the bow, and we all cheered through the frigid spray.

"Left forward hard! All forward hard!"

Our raft lunged out of the main current toward the starboard-side bank.

"There's another raft coming down behind us with a new guide. I want to make sure they get through."

A bright yellow raft with six paddlers and a greenhorn guide immediately rounded the bend.

"Uh oh," John said as we watched.

The yellow raft bounced off a boulder like a pinball and entered the first big drop sideways, sending the raft straight up in the air and ejecting all seven rafters. Arms, legs, and paddles flailed everywhere. One by one, each rafter surfaced. John had our raft head back out, and we assisted them through the current and into the eddy.

We beached the rafts. The last lady floating into the eddy had blood covering her face. John and her guide waded out and quickly pulled her into the eddy.

"Get me some ice from the cooler!" John commanded. Anastasia responded quickly with a plastic bag full.

"My leg really hurts," the lady whimpered. I guessed she was in her forties. I could see now she had a big gash on the bridge of her nose. They carried her up on the beach and took off her wetsuit booties, revealing a nasty swollen ankle.

They applied a compress to her face to stop the bleeding and ice to her ankle. Once the mayhem died down and they made plans to help this sweet lady back to camp for additional care, I overheard the exchange between our experienced guide and the dejected rookie.

"Man, I don't know how we missed that entrance." The young guide hung his head. "I'm pretty sure that was a paddle that caught her in the face. Ugh. I feel terrible. That's probably a broken nose with stitches and a broken ankle. Not a great record so far."

"I hear you, man. It happens. You know that feeling you have right now in your gut? Don't forget it. That brokenness will carve the awareness of your need right into your soul. Sometimes it's our own doing, sometimes it's from someone else's stupidity, and sometimes it's just life. Broken is broken. You probably had a weaker paddler on one side that didn't dig in. Stay low. Grow. Prepare. Revere the river. I think if you don't stay broken, it has a way of breaking you. Staying broken hurts less than being broken. As you can see, the stakes are high." John put his hand on the rookie's shoulder. "Great news, dude. The river allows us to continue writing the story every day. I like your ownership as a guide, but don't let this own you."

Let me hear joy and gladness;
   let the bones you have crushed rejoice.
      —PSALM 51:8

My sacrifice, O God, is a broken spirit;
   a broken and contrite heart
   you, God, will not despise.
      —PSALM 51:17

When Nathan the prophet came to King David and confronted him about his adultery and murder, it broke the king, who was a "man after God's own heart." His sin had found him out. There was no escape except through the door of repentance. He was made low in front of the holy of holies. In Psalm 51, we read of his utter devastation, repentance, and recognition of his need for God's forgiveness and restoration. His spiritual "bones" were crushed under the weight of his sin. This is where the beauty of God pours in. He restores us. We do not deserve it because of who we are or what we do. We receive his mercy and grace because of his character and nature. Brokenness is recognizing we are not whole without him.

Brokenness is a posture without pride, without self-reliance, knowing that we can't do anything to heal ourselves. It makes us completely dependent on Jesus.

We were born into a broken world. We are broken people with a broken nature. While it sounds hopeless at first, we know it's not! It's in the broken places of these earthen "jars of clay" that the healer shines through and restores. As those who guide people to experience God, it is paramount that we fundamentally operate from an acknowledgement and awareness of our weakness and his power.

John told the young guide, "If you don't stay broken, it has a way of breaking you." Staying broken means recognizing our need. It means recognizing we don't hold the power to fix ourselves or anyone else. If we don't continually recognize our need for God and his power, he will have to break that self-reliant pride. He loves us too much to let us worship at the throne of ourselves.

In chapter 9 of our study, we discussed the importance of character. This is an especially important topic for those who desire to lead others in worship. God is in the process of shaping and developing our character so that we conform to the image of his Son, Jesus. It turns out that one of God's main ways for developing character in us is through brokenness.

The way of worship will inevitably lead to a time of brokenness. A. W. Tozer asserts that "it is doubtful whether God can bless a man greatly until He has hurt him deeply."[1] Down through the centuries, practically every great servant of God has gone through a period of brokenness. A person may experience brokenness any number of ways.

First, brokenness may be experienced through an event, such as the death of a loved one, a divorce, bankruptcy, a serious automobile accident, a disappointing experience at work or the loss of a meaningful relationship.

Second, brokenness may also be the consequence of poor choices or sinful behavior, like sexual impropriety, addiction, self-centeredness, anger, dishonesty, or disobedience.

Third, brokenness may stem from some type of physical pain, like a chronic illness, terminal sickness, disease, a long hospital stay, a serious infirmity, or loss of physical ability.

But no matter how we enter this season of pain or sorrow, in order to be a worshiper, one must be broken. These times break us away from our own, personal motivating drive, will, or ambition and teach us to give total control, allegiance, obedience, and submission of our lives to Jesus. It *always* involves a renovation of attitude.

God is in the business of using broken people. Psalm 34:18 reminds us that "the LORD is close to the brokenhearted and saves those who are crushed in spirit," and "he heals the brokenhearted and binds up their wounds" (Ps 147:3). Whatever the circumstances, Jesus himself gives testimony of his mission to mend and heal the brokenhearted:

> He has sent Me to heal the brokenhearted,
> To proclaim liberty to the captives
> And recovery of sight to the blind,
> To set at liberty those who are oppressed;
> To proclaim the acceptable year of the Lord!
> —LUKE 4:18–19 NKJV

The story mentioned earlier about the prophet Nathan and King David from 2 Samuel 11–12 climaxes with King David repenting of his adulterous and murderous actions:

> You do not delight in sacrifice, or I would bring it;
>   you do not take pleasure in burnt offerings.
> My sacrifice, O God, is a broken spirit;
>   a broken and contrite heart
>   you, God, will not despise.
> —PSALM 51:16–17

What is meant by being broken in Spirit? And why does God demand a broken spirit and a contrite heart?

God takes us through the brokenness process so that he can shape and conform us into his image. Brokenness in spirit is more a condition of the heart than an action. Brokenness is not a sentiment, emotion, or special sensation. Brokenness is a heart attitude. God is in the business of changing attitudes. Brokenness in spirit transforms a self-centered, self-righteous, critical disposition into one of love, compassion, empathy, and kindheartedness. "Do nothing out of selfish ambition or vain conceit. Rather, in humility value others above yourselves" (Phil 2:3).

The prophet Jeremiah submits himself to the mighty hand of God and through his times of brokenness, he is shaped and fashioned into a faithful worshiper. During this process, he is given a poignant picture illustrating why the brokenness was necessary.

God instructs Jeremiah to go down to the potter's house:

> This is the word that came to Jeremiah from the Lord: "Go down to the potter's house, and there I will give you my message." So I went down to the potter's house, and I saw him working at the wheel. But the pot he was shaping from the clay was marred in his hands; so the potter formed it into another pot, shaping it as seemed best to him.
>
> Then the word of the Lord came to me . . . "Like clay in the hand of the potter, so are you in my hand, Israel"
>
> —JEREMIAH 18:1–6

The psalmist says, "I have become like broken pottery" (Ps 31:12). And just like a vessel in the potter's hand, repairing broken pieces, shaping and modeling on a turning wheel, God wants to refashion our broken lives into vessels fit for his service. Our personalities, character, integrity, strengths and weaknesses, likes and dislikes all combine to form clay in God's almighty hands. And just as earthen clay and chemicals react to the fire and environment of a kiln, our worship and times of brokenness reveal and shape our true character. As we respond to the cultural fires, social influences, and hedonistic pressures around us, God takes our gifts of worship—our heart of love for the Lord—and shapes us into acceptable vessels of worship and praise.

Mildred Witte Struven once said, "A clay pot sitting in the sun will always be a clay pot. It has to go through the white heat of the furnace to become porcelain."[2] Likewise, when our worship is marred by the chemical imbalances of this world, the evil influences of a carnal culture, and the self-centeredness of ego, God has to break us and reshape us into new vessels. He places us in the fiery kiln and permits us to confront life experiences—trials, hardship, persecution, and at times suffering. His process of breaking and reshaping makes us better and stronger worshipers.

You see, once we as broken vessels are repaired, reshaped, and reformed in his image, God places the glaze of the Holy Spirit upon our lives and creates a totally different texture, a new vessel. He reshapes our desires. Like pottery refashioned and made anew as reliable basins of honor, we too take on new character, develop a reliable finish, and become useful to his kingdom.

But this process can take a long time. To be broken in Spirit means we live a life of abandonment to the Holy Spirit. The Holy Spirit controls our motives, desires, ambitions, attitudes, and aspirations. Brokenness involves surrender, submission, compliance, and acquiescence to the work of the Holy Spirit. In one true sense, as Harold Vaughan said, "brokenness is the shattering of my will so that all my responses are filled with the Holy Spirit."[3] Duncan Campbell said, "If you are filled with the Holy Spirit you can't be filled with anything else."[4] This kind of brokenness is deliberate, transforming, and life-changing. It involves a pouring out of self and sin from the secret chambers of the heart. Humbleness replaces arrogance. Tenderheartedness replaces selfish, self-centered ego. Kindness replaces bitterness and retaliation. God literally transforms us from the inside out.

Though brokenness confronts us with how weak we are, ultimately, it leads us into a place of greater spiritual power and freedom, no matter the difficulty and struggle. Most often, the experience of being broken gives us a new perspective. There is a renewed willingness to confront issues of the heart and a readiness to be broken of sin and disobedience. God uses circumstances and presses in on us for the sole purpose of shaping our ambitions, molding character and infusing into the heart a deeper desire for fellowship, mentoring, and friendship with himself.

I never cease to be amazed at how those of us given the charge and responsibility of leading worship can so easily become arrogant and prideful in assuming what is most assuredly a "humble task"— worship. And when we find ourselves getting too self-assured, too full of ourselves, too boastful and conceited, God most often brings us to a place of brokenness. Several years ago, God brought me to such a place of brokenness in my life journey. I had experienced a long season of success in developing a large and fruitful center for worship. Hundreds of students were responding to the worship training programs I had designed. Scores of young men and women that I had personally trained were assuming full-time positions in some of the most influential churches in America. From the outside, all looked really good. I'm not sure I was really aware of it at the time, but if truth be told, I was very proud of what had been accomplished in the training of worship leaders over such a relatively short period of time.

Then, one Sunday morning, on the way home from leading worship in my local church, I was involved in a very serious, life-threatening car accident. Both of my legs were broken. My left ankle was shattered into a hundred pieces. And for more than six months, I lay helpless in a hospital bed. I could not walk. All of the mobility I had taken for granted was gone. I went from running full speed in every area of my life to . . . stop! God literally shut me down. And for the next many days and months, God used sleepless nights, lonely hours, the truth of his Word, and the desperate fear of the unknown to break my haughty, arrogant spirit. His Holy Spirit placed the spotlight of conviction and condemnation on my dark heart and revealed the seriousness of my sin. After more than a dozen surgeries, a serious bout with staph infection, and accepting the reality that, barring a miracle from God, I was facing certain death, I learned the lessons of being broken in spirit, broken of self, and the need to be totally broken and surrendered to God and his working in my life.

It was this one area of sin, perhaps more than any other, that was refined out of me through the brokenness experience: pride. The apostle James reminds us that "God opposes the proud, but shows favor to the humble" (James 4:6). I most immediately stopped bragging on what I had accomplished and began following the biblical instruction to "let someone else praise you, and not your own mouth; an outsider, and not your own lips" (Prov 27:2).

In reality, brokenness and humility do not, will not, and cannot coexist with pride, self-centered arrogance, and egotism. Pride goes before destruction and a haughty spirit before a fall (Prov 16:18). Before destruction, the heart of a man is haughty, and before honor is humility (Prov 18:12). The Bible declares that "a haughty look, a proud heart, *And* the plowing of the wicked *are sin*" (Prov 21:4 NKJV; emphasis added). The brokenness experience will purge a person of conceit, egotism, superiority complexes, and pride.

Do you struggle with the sin of arrogance? Are there times in your life and in your relationships with people where you genuinely feel a sense of superiority? Do you wrestle in the inner part of your heart with a spirit of condescension toward the marginalized and less fortunate?

When one is broken in spirit, the Holy Spirit removes any disposition of arrogance, smugness, self-importance, ego, and conceit. Those following the way of worship must follow the teaching of Philippians

2:3 to esteem others above ourselves with lowliness of mind, humility, and submission.

So what is the final outcome of brokenness? God uses his Word and the circumstances we are going through to break us. How we respond to these pressures reveals to the world our true character. Do these pressures make us bitter or better? Does our song become one of humility and submission? When we humble ourselves under the mighty hand of God, he promises to exalt, restore, and equip us for a lifetime of service (1 Pet 5:6–7). After this time of brokenness, are we able to successfully deal with the victory that comes with the new, lofty position God now places us in?

There are a few ways we can recognize the work of God in our broken places.

First, brokenness is transformational. God uses brokenness to renovate us as worshipers. The Holy Spirit changes disposition, demeanor, and deportment—our attitudes—from self-serving to Christ-proclaiming.

Second, brokenness most often gives us opportunity to restore fractured relationships. His Holy Spirit converts and modifies our inclination toward condescension and exclusivity into a heart attitude filled with acceptance, approval, and inclusion—preferring others before ourselves.

Third, the brokenness experience gives us renewed vision for God's mission and purposes in our life. We say with the great New Testament apostle, "I have been crucified with Christ and I no longer live, but Christ lives in me. The *life* I now live in the body, I live by faith in the Son of God, who loved me and gave himself for me" (Gal 2:20; emphasis added). Harold Vaughn says,

A man who is crucified with Christ has no right to self-pity, bitterness, or retaliation. Since dead men have no rights, there is no place for fighting, fuming, fretting, or complaining in this blood-bought temple.

When I am broken, I have nothing to lose and nothing to prove. There is tremendous rest in being crucified with Christ.[5]

Fourth, God often uses the brokenness experience to prepare us for a meaningful position of leadership. But this is always in his time and for his intentions (1 Pet 5:6).

Jesus said,

Whoever wants to become great among you must be your servant, and whoever wants to be first must be slave of all. For even the Son of Man did not come to be served, but to serve, and to give his life as a ransom for many.

—MARK 10:43–45

The position of leadership God has for us may not look like what we think of as important or prestigious, but it will be significant and meaningful in his eyes. The power of the position will be undeniably from the Holy Spirit.

To review the "brokenness principle," it is doubtful that anyone seeking the way of worship will ever worship genuinely until that person has experienced a season of brokenness. And Jesus gives testimony that he came to mend the brokenhearted.

So what are the lessons taught by brokenness for those seeking the way of worship?

1. God uses *brokenness to transform us from the inside out!* Faithful worshiper, I don't know your situation or the struggles you are facing individually, in your family, or with deciding to be obedient to what you believe God has called you to do in life. But I do know that I serve a God that is still in the business of healing broken hearts, mending broken marriages, healing broken bones, and restoring broken relationships. Don't be distracted or stumble over the difficult circumstances you are facing today.

2. *Remember, brokenness most often gives us opportunity to restore fractured relationships.* It is truly amazing how God can make broken relationships whole. He can transform disappointing situations into opportunities for showing his grace. Faithful soldier, I am certain God will use the difficult situation you may be facing to help mold and transform you into his image.

3. *The brokenness experience will give you renewed vision for God's mission and purposes in your life!* Brokenhearted pilgrim, be assured of this! God already knows your heart's desire, and he stands ready for you to take your burden to the cross, lay that burden down, and leave it at his feet.

4. *God often uses the brokenness experience to prepare you and me for a meaningful position of leadership.* Trust God. Give your burdens to Jesus. And watch him do a miracle work in your heart—every time. And in the words of Oswald Chambers, "Get to the end of yourself where you can do nothing; but where he does everything!"[6]

CHAPTER 12

HUMILITY

"Who's hungry? John asked as we eased down a calm stretch of the river.

"Starved!"

"Famished!"

"I'm about to eat my rubbah bootie!" Neal chimed in with the rest of us.

The noonday sun warmed the canyon perfectly. A splash of the fifty-degree water on the back of the neck was invigorating.

"There's something about being outside in the fresh air and on the water that makes me so hungry," Leah commented.

"I don't need fresh air or water. I wake up hungry. I go to sleep hungry. I stay hungry. It's one of my greatest strengths." Neal was non-stop with the jokes.

We guided the raft up onto the pebbled beach and hoisted ourselves out. There was a long stretch of sandy clay shore with a few stumps and logs strewn about and an old campfire site with vertical log seats surrounding it. It felt good to stretch our legs and be on dry ground for a bit.

"Guys, you see that trail at the mouth of the woods?" John pointed. "If you follow that for about ten minutes or so there's a beautiful vista. Mike, you can lead the way."

I pointed to my chest and raised my eyebrows.

"Yep. Just grab the bear spray out of my dry bag."

"I thought we were stopping to *have* lunch, not *be* lunch," I said nervously.

"You'll be fine," John said. "In fact, Anastasia can take you guys. Everything should be ready here in a few minutes."

"You need any help?" I tried to get out of the "don't get eaten by a bear" hike.

"No, you guys just go enjoy the view and relax. I got this," John replied.

The apprentice guide led us down the narrow, well-worn path under the canopy of fir, pine, and juniper trees. Her white, corn-silk hair bounced as she traipsed ahead of us. The occasional chirp of chickadees and finches against the faint roar of whitewater was all we could hear. No roaring cars or machinery, just nature. Every bit of this place was magical to us Floridians.

After a brief hike of ups and downs, the forest opened up, and the roar of the whitewater overtook our conversation. We stepped out onto an overlook of thunderous rapids that churned a couple of stories below.

"Wow, are we rafting that?" Franny asked.

"Oh yes. It's not so bad. It's really fun!" Anastasia responded. "The river is beautiful from every angle, isn't it?"

After a few minutes of taking in the magnificent view, we headed back. As we arrived at the beach, we found John putting the final touches on lunch for us. I was taken aback by his attention to detail and hospitality.

"These are roast beef with horseradish cheddar, and these are smoked turkey and provolone with my homemade pesto spread."

He pointed at the different options. "The butter, lettuce, and tomatoes are from my garden, by the way. I cut up some fresh fruit over there, and you can choose your drink from the cooler."

"Are you married?" Franny asked as she refreshed her lipstick.

"I'm right here!" Neal responded.

We dug into the delicious food and enjoyed each other's company.

"Wow man, thanks for this," I commented quietly to John. "We could've helped."

His reply stuck with me.

"No way, man, I just want you guys to enjoy the river. It's my pleasure, really. My grandpa used to say, 'Stay low, John. Stay low. This whole thing ain't about you. Disappear into the river. The joy in life is in thinking about others more than yourself.' My job is to serve you, period. Let's eat!"

Do nothing out of selfish ambition or vain conceit. Rather, in humility value others above yourselves, not looking to your own interests but each of you to the interests of the others.

—PHILIPPIANS 2:3–4

"Stay low." What a statement from an incredible athlete, an expert in his field. He was strong, good-looking, confident, and a leader. How does a person like that stay low when everything in our culture says, "Elevate yourself"? Our human nature clamors for approval, notoriety, power, and influence. It's survival of the fittest. The most visible, the strongest, the prettiest, or the most important person wins, right?

John just wanted us to experience the river. He prepared for us. He thought of us even before we started our trip. He looked after our safety and experience. He allowed us to view the vista and majesty of the river while he prepared a meal. Isn't this what we as worship leaders should do?

Andrew Murray said, "Pride must die in you, or nothing of heaven can live in you."[1]

If you are a lead worshiper, guiding people into his presence, there is a war you must wage. It's a war against the accolades of men and the enthronement of ourselves upon our hearts. It's a battle against our pride and selfish ambition. It's a war against the futility of fame, however large our influence. Pride knows no audience too small. We've seen the humility of the highly visible and famous, and we've witnessed the stifling pride of one whose platform is only a few. We share art that moves people. The lights are on us. The cameras are on us. We must wrestle and war against self-aggrandizement. We are to stay low. But humility is a funny thing. It's a slippery trait. Once you think you've achieved it, you don't have it anymore. We are to point to the only one worthy of our highest praise. At the end of the day, the one we worship, Jesus, has shown us the way. He is the epitome of humility, the pinnacle of selflessness, and the one who gives us the grace to stay low.

> In your relationships with one another, have the same mindset as Christ Jesus: Who, being in very nature God, did not consider equality with God something to be used to his own advantage; rather, he made himself nothing by taking the very nature of a servant, being made in human likeness. And being found in appearance as a man, he humbled himself by becoming obedient to death—even death on a cross!
>
> —PHILIPPIANS 2:5–8

In the previous chapters, we've discussed many essential traits for worship leaders—thankfulness, character, brokenness. When we explore these issues, we quickly find aspects of our own hearts that can hinder the free expression of honest worship.

Among these many crucial characteristics, humility may be one of the most important. This word refers to an attitude and an action, perception and pattern, or disposition and deportment. The Old Testament rendering for the word *humble* involves two Hebrew words, *'anav*[2] or *shâphâl*.[3] The first translates "poor, afflicted, or meek" and is used in Numbers 12:3 to describe Moses as "a very humble man, more humble than anyone else on the face of the earth." The writer is describing Moses's disposition, the attitude of his heart.

While the second also speaks of a heart condition, it is used more in terms of an action and in opposition to pride or haughtiness. It implies being ranked below others who are honored or rewarded, to have a modest opinion of one's self, or to behave in an unassuming manner. It's used in Isaiah 57:15, 18–19 and defines the person that demonstrates a contrite or humble spirit:

> For this is what the high and exalted One says—
>> he who lives forever, whose name is holy:
> "I live in a high and holy place,
>> but also with the one who is contrite and lowly in spirit,
> to revive the spirit of the lowly
>> and to revive the heart of the contrite. . . .
> I have seen their ways, but I will heal them;
>> I will guide them and restore comfort to Israel's mourners,
> creating praise on their lips.
> Peace, peace, to those far and near,"
>> says the Lord. "And I will heal them."
>> —ISAIAH 57:15, 18–19; EMPHASIS ADDED

This Hebrew word for "humble, humbled, or humility" occurs forty-three times in the New King James Version.[4] The Old Testament position is clear and most often stands in opposition to an attitude or spirit of pride, arrogance, or haughtiness. Proverbs 18:12 explains the importance of a humble disposition: "Before destruction the heart of a man is haughty, And before honor is humility" (NKJV). And Proverbs 22:4 clearly links the attitude with a respect or fear of the Lord: "Humility is the fear of the Lord; its wages are riches and honor and life" (emphasis added).

The New Testament is equally precise in its treatment of the word. It is from the Greek word *tapeinóō* and describes the choice to bring low or humble oneself.[5] This is the word the apostle Paul uses to describe a condition of the heart ("in humility value others above yourselves"; Phil 2:3) and an action ("He [Jesus] humbled himself by becoming obedient to death"; Phil 2:8) to be observed.[6] It describes a person who is unpretentious, modest, meek, or unassuming.

It can describe people who lower themselves in order to serve others, choose simplicity and respect over acclaim, or put themselves below others.[7] As a verb, it may describe the choice to "reduce in power, to make lowly in mind; to abase the pride or arrogance of; reduce the self-sufficiency of; to destroy the independence, power, or will of; or make submissive." It is with this application in mind that the apostle Peter instructs young believers to "humble yourselves, therefore, under God's mighty hand, that he may lift you up in due time" (1 Pet 5:6).[8]

So what does humility have to do with the way of worship? Humility reflects the motives of our heart. There are four main ways this applies to those of us given the responsibility to lead worship.

First, humility confirms a sense of calling. When a person answers the call to lead God's people in worship, there comes an immediate commitment to a life of humility. Worship is always a reflection of the heart. God is not looking for haughty, arrogant, know-it-all worship leaders to stand before his church and proclaim the day of the Lord.

He is not seeking the services of a prideful person filled with ego and self-centered agendas and motives. God is looking for musicians who want to serve. He is looking for men and women with a contrite spirit. He is looking for worship leaders that can lead with the power of the Holy Spirit on their lives. He is looking for men and women with hearts of love that reverently fear God with humility.

Second, humility provides the platform to feel secure in the role of worship. Being a qualified worship guide has more to do with the heart than with musical prowess or great skill as a communicator. Of course, musicianship, talent, skill, and ability are important. But talent and skill alone will not garner the blessings of the Holy Spirit upon a worship leader's ministry. Neither will they reap the joys of training and equipping others so that they too can lead worship. God is looking for musicians who have a deep, abiding passion to lead worshipers into a meaningful relationship with Jesus, and this is primarily *others-focused*. The foundational qualifications for the spirit-filled worship leader begin with the ability to demonstrate a genuine, humble, servant-leadership attitude. It has been said that the best way to stand up before the world is to kneel down before God. This kind of posture requires a life of surrender, and it comes with immediate benefits and blessings.

Third, humility is a reflection of the heart's motive. James Packer says, "The healthy heart is one that bows down in humility and rises in praise and adoration."[9] Humility revives the spirit of the humble and the heart of the contrite one (Isa 57:15). Songwriter Darlene Zschech puts the worship of God and the role of the humble in perspective:

> The humble worship God, love to see and hear others worship God, and experience the presence of God in worship. Anyone who is proud and arrogant cannot stand to hear the Father, Son and Holy Spirit being worshipped, but the humble love to worship Him and also to hear others worship Him.[10]

Fourth, humility is shaped by obedience. Perhaps the greatest example of humility is Jesus. He humbled himself and became obedient (Phil 2:8). Obedience is the true and honest result of being humble in spirit. It is also one of the greatest gauges of biblical worship.

In the final analysis, humility guards your heart from the constant call toward pride, self-centeredness, and arrogance. While the arrogant can only look to themselves, the humble listen to a different, holy voice. They understand that "pride is the complete anti-God state of mind."[11] They have a unique and genuine awareness and Holy Spirit–led sense—their worship springs from a genuine love for Jesus. They align their life goals, blueprint for worship, and ambitions with an earnest desire to be clothed with humility (1 Pet 5:5). They have learned the joy of humbling themselves under the mighty hand of God and trust him for a holy outcome.

Humble worship leaders elevate the Lord's glory over their own talents and take every opportunity to direct people's minds toward God. Humble worship leaders don't show off how good their own voices are, how skilled they are, how gifted they are as a songwriter, or even how spiritual they are. Rather, humble worship leaders try to fade into the background as much as possible, recognizing that this moment is only about Jesus. Humble worship leaders don't treat worship as a performance but as an opportunity and privilege to communicate the truth as directed by the Holy Spirit.

Humility of heart provides a healthy perspective for those called to lead God's people in worship. Worship leaders captured by the Word of God will use strategic moments of collective adoration to reach out to the humble in heart. They will in humility value others above themselves (Phil 2:3). They will not harbor jealousy or envy when others are leading worship but exhibit the spirit of Philippians 2:3 to be humble and freely give honor to others.

CHAPTER 13

INTEGRITY

We finished up the delectable sandwiches John served us and mused about the first few hours of our trip.

"What's your favorite part so far, guys?" John asked as he brushed his hands off and finished chewing his last bite.

"I love it all," Leah said quickly. "I mean the scenery, the river, just being outside, it's all my favorite."

"The sandwiches, definitely the sandwiches," Neal quipped.

"I loved the first part of the morning, when we first put the raft in, and the mist was rising off the river. It's like the canyon was coming awake," Anastasia said in her Nordic accent.

We continued the conversation as we began cleaning up the site and preparing to get back on the water. John called us together.

"Hey guys, as you're putting your PFDs back on, let's circle up. I need to go over a few things with you regarding some rapids we'll hit in the next hour or so."

We formed a small semicircle.

"Just beyond that ridge way over there is a rapid we call the widow-maker." He pointed and gestured as he spoke. "We won't hit it for a while, but I wanted to give you a heads up. It's imperative you guys really pay attention and follow all my commands. So yesterday . . . uh . . . I'm not sure I should . . . " He rubbed his face with both hands and looked at Anastasia. After a few seconds and a sigh he continued.

"Here's the deal, guys. A twenty-one-year-old man died yesterday in the widow-maker."

He certainly had our attention. I saw the blood drain from a few faces. We all felt the weight of what he said.

"I thought this was supposed to be safe," Franny said.

"It is, if you know what you're doing. However, this is the wild, and nothing is 100 percent risk free."

"Should we go down that part of the river?" I asked.

"Look, we'll be fine, guys. If you follow me, we'll be fine. Okay?"

Everyone nodded nervously.

"Apparently, the guide from that raft put his rafters in jeopardy. He was with another company. Word is he had a shoulder injury or something that may have prevented him from steering properly, and when the kid fell out, he didn't follow protocol. Who knows if that guide actually coached him well or if he just panicked. It sounds like once he fell in, he fought the whitewater instead of letting it take him. He tried to climb up on a rock over and over until he exhausted himself, and he just got pinned in the keeper."

"What's a keeper?" I asked.

"The water pours down into a large crevice in the riverbed, and with a giant wave it folds back on itself and just keeps churning. It keeps anything that falls into it. Hence, a keeper."

"Man, I wouldn't want to be that guide," I commented. "The guilt alone would be crushing."

"Yeah, it's one thing when an accident happens. It's a whole other thing when you present yourself as healthy and ready to roll, and you aren't. He has probably disqualified himself from guiding commercially. At any rate, I've rafted this rapid hundreds of times and never had an issue. We'll be fine!"

Everyone flashed a nervous grin as we broke from our huddle and took our places in our rubber vessel.

The integrity of the upright guides them,
but the unfaithful are destroyed by their duplicity.
—PROVERBS 11:3

Our word *integrity* comes from the Latin word *integer*, which means "whole, complete, or one." Having integrity means you are a whole person or of one mind. To be a person of integrity means you are one person all the time. The opposite of a person of integrity is a duplicitous or divided person. Having integrity means you are governed by the same morals, principles, and values in every situation. In short, to possess integrity is to be the same person in public as we are in private. It is to not talk out of both sides of our mouths but rather be one in our representation. It is to hold fast to our convictions and not compromise them for any reason.

Opportunities abound for us to shade a conversation in our favor, oversell an opportunity to win someone over, or cover the tracks of secret sin and selfish ambition. Scripture tells us over and over that this will always lead to ruin. It will destroy our lives and our testimony, and it will detonate a bomb of destruction in the lives and ministries we lead.

Proverbs 4:23 says, "Above all else, guard your heart, for everything you do flows from it."

In our story, a young man lost his life in large part because a self-serving guide decided to move into the deep and dangerous waters while unhealthy and unprepared.

How many times have we seen leaders who lead publicly with great charisma be brought to rubble by decisions made from a fractured soul? It would have been better for that guide to say, "I'm not well, I better not lead anyone right now." He could have gotten treatment and moved toward wholeness. The story would have ended very differently. Maybe he thought he needed the money. Maybe he didn't want to be thought of as weak. Whatever the rationale, it wasn't worth it.

Our integrity is a sacred offering of worship. Living as one, being undivided in our convictions, is the foundation by which we can live and lead in freedom and strength. We must fortify the walls of our integrity daily. It must be intentional. We will not drift toward oneness, but by God's grace, we can be ever paddling toward it. We must allow the Word of truth, the power of the Holy Spirit, and the fellowship of trusted brothers and sisters living in the light together hold us accountable.

It's a clarion call to all of us, out of love for our Savior, to tend to our integrity as though our lives, and the lives of those we lead, depend on it. Because they do.

Being a worship leader requires a life of integrity. Along with character, brokenness, and humility, integrity is part of the unseen fabric that resides deep within a person. In one sense, these are pillars that support the life given to worship.

1. **Character** refers to "being everything one claims to be."
2. **Brokenness** refers to circumstances and experiences for testing one's character.
3. **Humility** is the absolute removal of the spirit of selfishness and pride.
4. **Integrity** refers to being sound, whole, and complete.

These qualities are at times so deeply interrelated in a life of worship that they are difficult to view separately. But they are individually important. For example, there is a difference between integrity and character: "**Character** is one's moral and ethical code, and **integrity** [refers to] one [who] lives according to that code."[1]

In Hebrew, integrity refers to wholeness of mind, innocence, and a lack of evil purpose. Integrity could mean you don't have an ulterior motive, or that you are upright or perfect. In the Old Testament, the Hebrew word *tom* is translated as "fullness, innocence, simplicity, or integrity." In the King James Version, it occurs sixteen times. This word is translated eleven times as *integrity*; six times as *upright, uprightly, or uprightness*; four times as *venture or full*; and once each for *perfection, perfect, or simplicity*. This is the same word for integrity used to describe God's heart when Abraham falsely represented Sarah as his sister (Gen 20:5–6); to instruct Solomon's walk before the Lord, even as his father King David walked in integrity (1 Kgs 9:4); to commend the upright in Proverbs (Prov 11:3; 19:1; 20:7); and to command worshipers to come before the Lord with an honest heart in Psalm 96 (Pss 7:8; 25:21; 26:1, 11; 41:12; 78:72).

Consider the following illustration. On Wednesday, August 1, 2007, at 6:05 p.m., during the evening rush hour, the main spans of the I-35W Mississippi River bridge in Minneapolis, Minnesota, collapsed. Built in 1967, the 1,907-foot steel truss arched bridge was Minnesota's fifth-busiest, carrying more than 140,000 vehicles daily. Thirteen people died, and about one hundred more were injured. The eight-lane bridge was one of the two major river crossings of I-35W in Minnesota. At 6:05 p.m., with rush hour traffic moving slowly across the bridge, the central span of the structure suddenly gave way. The deck collapsed into the river, the south part falling more than eighty-one feet.

The civil engineering department of the University of Minnesota had done a study as early as 2001 and discovered a deficiency with the cross girders at the end of the approach spans. In 2005, the bridge was again rated as "structurally deficient." Again, on June 15, 2006, the U.S. Department of Transportation noted problems of cracking and fatigue with the structure. Simply put, the bridge's integrity was in serious question. In fact, its integrity was compromised. The structure would not and could not do that for which it was designed. And the consequences were extreme.[2]

Integrity has everything to do with reliability. Any compromises of integrity in the construction process when building a bridge, airplane, or automobile can potentially have dangerous, fatal consequences. When we step onto a commercial airplane, we trust the integrity of the pilot to do the job and the equipment to be reliable and safe. When we drive our cars, we trust in the integrity of the engine to start and the vehicle to get us to our destination. The credibility of life insurance is based on the company's integrity to deliver at the time of need.

The same is true for those seeking to follow the way of worship. The credibility of a person's worship is based on individual integrity. Just as the integrity of a bridge ensures the safety of those crossing, the integrity of a person leading worship means he or she is spiritually reliable. To the extent that a person's ethics, character, morality, brokenness, and humility are integrated, that person has integrity. Only then can a person's integrity enable him or her to present honest, genuine, and Holy-Spirit sanctioned worship.

Our integrity is a sacred offering of worship. Integrity reflects the purpose, substance, and consistency of our public and private praise. After all, when we lead corporate worship, we serve as called-out agents to bring sacrifices of praise to God. Any time the body of Christ approaches special times of worship, they must trust the credibility of the worship leader's integrity. Worship leaders offer sacrifices of praise to the Lord on behalf of all the people. Their commitment to honesty, truthfulness, honor, reliability, and uprightness as worshipers inevitably exposes their heart dedication, motive, and personal commitment to worship integrity.

Our integrity sets the standard for our worship. While the spiritual and moral issues of worship—doing right, giving your best, and completing the task—are important, the worshiper's commitment to always give the Lord the best of the best is just as important. The brothers and sisters at the young church at Colossae were reminded, "Whatever you do, work at it with all your heart, as working for the Lord, not for human masters. . . . It is the Lord Christ you are serving" (Col 3:23–24). Oswald Chambers puts the principle in perspective this way:

Whenever [our rights are] made the guidance in life, it will blunt the spiritual insight. The great enemy of the life of faith in God is not sin, but the good which is not good enough. The good is always the enemy of the best.[3]

Our integrity regulates the accountability of our worship. While the Holy Spirit is actually the one that holds us accountable for our heart's intentions, ambitions, and actions, it is our commitment to integrity—doing right with all our heart, life, and mind—that ensures pure, upright, godly behavior without ulterior motive or agenda. Rick Warren reminds us that "integrity is built by defeating the temptation to be dishonest."[4] This kind of integrity compels the worshiper to flee hypocrisy, do justly, love mercy, walk humbly (Micah 6:8), and follow the pattern of good works for the testimony of Jesus Christ:

In everything set them an example by *doing* what is good. In your teaching *show* integrity, seriousness and soundness of speech that cannot be condemned, so that those who oppose you may be ashamed because they have nothing bad to say about us.
—TITUS 2:7–8; EMPHASIS ADDED

As worship leaders, our testimony should be that of Asaph's contemplation as he wrote about God's kindness to rebellious Israel.

Speaking of the Lord's integrity of heart, Asaph writes, "So [God] shepherded them according to the *integrity* of his heart, and guided them by the skillfulness of his hands" (Psalm 78:72 NKJV; emphasis added).

We need to submit ourselves as worshipers to the integrity of God's heart. We need to follow Asaph's lead and worship with the skill and passion of men and women committed to a life of integrity. Our worship should be led with character compelled by obedience and prompted by sacrifices of praise, remembering that if we are committed to living out our worship through obedience, then we will naturally demonstrate our sacrifice of praise with integrity.

CHAPTER 14

LIVING WATER

During a docile stretch of water, we floated along as if on a slow conveyor belt. Occasionally John would gently rotate us so that we got a 360-degree view of the canyon.

"What are you thinking about?" Leah asked me that often, as I tend to get lost in my thoughts. "You've been quiet for a while, just staring off. Just make sure you don't miss this."

She's good for me. Even just four years into our still-developing marriage, she knew me well. I tend to sink deep into thought about shaping our future, building a good life, or some creative initiative that I hope will change the world. While she loves and appreciates how God has wired me, she continually brings me into the present.

"I'm just taking it all in, actually. It's so much more than I expected. I've also been thinking about something John said earlier this morning."

"I knew there was something. What did he say?" Leah asked. We spoke quietly, as the others were conversing about the weather.

"When Neal asked him if this was all he did, John said, 'Why would I need anything else? Once you experience the river . . . you live.' I'm curious about what that really meant."

"I can tell you what that meant," John said as he flashed a huge grin.

How in the world did he hear us with everyone else talking?

I smiled back, a little embarrassed that he overheard our conversation. "Absolutely, man. I'd love to hear more about that. It sounded pretty deep."

"I don't know how deep it actually is, but it's deep for me. There was a time a few years ago when I wanted out of the family business. My dad and I had it out, so I took off. I was exploring, traveling, getting into some bad stuff. I was searching for the meaning of it all, I guess. I ended up pretty bankrupt in every way, not just financially. My search brought me nothing but heartache. The short version of it is, I came back. My dad is incredible. He welcomed me back. This time I actually surrendered to him and to my destiny with the river. That's when I got serious about becoming one with the river, and everything settled for me. I was finally at rest. I was satisfied, no longer aching for something else to bring me joy and purpose. I didn't need to chase anything else. It's all found in the river for me."

"Wow, man. That's amazing." I paused for a minute, then I had to ask. "So does that mean you never leave and do other things?"

"No not at all. It means the river never leaves me. See, I raft rivers all over the world. I travel and explore. It just means I'm satisfied. I don't need to chase other things . . . money, relationships, power, influence. I'm good. I'm just good."

Jesus answered, "Everyone who drinks this water will be thirsty again, but whoever drinks the water I give them will never thirst. Indeed, the water I give them will become in them a spring of water welling

up to eternal life." The woman said to him, "Sir, give me this water so
that I won't get thirsty and have to keep coming here to draw water."
—JOHN 4:13–15

The way of worship says, "I know where my source of life comes from."
Jesus offers himself as a spring of water that never runs dry. His spirit,
his life—he completely satisfies. When we drink from the wells of
earthly pursuits, we still thirst. When we try to find our worth in
the accolades of others, the pursuit of fleeting lusts, or in comfort or
power, we come up empty. Every other "god" will disappoint us. Jesus
is the only one worthy. He is our living water. When we believe and
surrender to him, he is the geyser, the spring of life, love, and joy that
erupts from within forever.

There have been times in my life I've drifted to search for significance in my achievement or the approval of leaders I revered.
No longer. While we must steward well the gifts God has put in our
hands, the influence or achievement of those efforts must not be the
goal. If it is, we will still thirst. It is important to serve our authori-
ties with grateful effort, but we cannot rest our worth in the praise
of men.

If we do, we will still thirst.

Jesus says, "I am more than enough." He is the living water, the
river of life that never runs dry. He is the fountain of forgiveness and
worth. John said he was "finally at rest" and "no longer aching for
something else." We must rest and drink in the fountain of Jesus.
You will never be thirsty again.

On the last and greatest day of the festival, Jesus stood and said
in a loud voice, "Let anyone who is thirsty come to me and drink.
Whoever believes in me, as Scripture has said, rivers of living water
will flow from within them."
—JOHN 7:37–38

In this chapter, we see Jesus is the *living water* that forever satisfies every spiritual need. This water flows in and through our lives as a wellspring of life. In the two passages cited above (John 4:13–15 and John 7:37–38), Jesus uses the word *thirst* to describe a basic *human* desire, craving, or necessity. But Jesus is not speaking of a physical, human thirst. He is focusing on spiritual thirst—as in "My soul thirsts for You, my flesh longs for You in a dry and weary land where there is no water" (Ps 63:1 NKJV). And "spiritual thirst is a picture of one of our greatest physical needs, water."[1] Humans can live several days without food, but they cannot survive long without water.

We have all experienced physical thirst (Greek: *dipsaō*) on a hot day. But the word can refer to any "strong or eager desire." We can thirst for knowledge, righteousness, power, or control. This word is used strategically in six biblical passages to denote those individuals who "painfully feel and eagerly long for things by which the soul is refreshed, supported or strengthened."[2]

The exact same Greek word appears in John 4:13; 6:35; 7:37; Revelation 7:16; 21:6; and 22:17 in the context of an invitation or provocation. In speaking to a Samaritan woman (John 4:13) about the "gift of God," Jesus introduces "living water" as an antidote to thirst and depicts a dynamic, eternal relationship. In John 6:35, Jesus declares that he is "the bread of life," and any person placing full confidence in him will never thirst.[3] In John 7:37, Jesus issues an invitation so that *anyone who is thirsty* may be the recipient of living water flowing up from within. In John 4:13–15 and 7:37–39, Jesus again uses the term "living water" to illustrate a deeply personal, spiritual commodity. In this context, "living" describes the quality of a powerfully strong and vigorous relationship that is both enriching and eternal.[4]

Five statements found in John 4:10–15 are important to those seeking the way of worship. Jesus makes two pronouncements as part of a personal invitation to a Samaritan woman, and three in John 7:37–38 as part of a public invitation. These two passages help us understand why Jesus uses this analogy of living water.

Personal Invitation

In this story, Jesus meets a woman from the little country of Samaria at Jacob's Well, a place of extraordinary historical significance. Jesus asks the woman for a drink of water. She is a bit rattled by the inquiry because Jews and Samaritans rarely interacted with each other.

Undaunted by her reaction, Jesus continues to converse with her. When the woman notices that he has nothing to use to draw water from the well, Jesus makes his first pronouncement, forever changing the woman's life.

He says anyone "who drinks this water will be thirsty again, but whoever drinks the water I give them will never thirst" (John 4:13–14).

Jesus seeks to meet a deeply personal, spiritual need in the woman's heart. At this point, she only sees how her physical needs may be met. "Sir," she says, "give me this water so that I won't get thirsty and have to keep coming here to draw water" (John 4:15). But Jesus knows that inside of every person is a thirst that can never be satisfied by the promises of this world—fame, success, sexual satisfaction, wealth, intellectual pursuit, career advancement, significance, or happiness.[5] "The only real thirst quencher of our parched soul is Jesus because he alone is the giver of living water."[6] It is important to note that physical water never satisfies soul thirst. Only Jesus—the living water—can satisfy a thirsty soul.

Jesus then reaches out to the woman at the place of her greatest need with his second invitation for living water, saying, "the water I give them will become in them a spring of water welling up to eternal life." (John 4:14).

Jesus is offering the Samaritan woman eternal life. He explains how the "living water" he is offering will spring up (*hallomai* = "leap up, gush, or rejoice") within her. This is a metaphor for the "Holy Spirit bursting forth like a well with no boundaries, no limits. And it continues to spring from the inside out," Ken Boa says.[7] Oswald Chambers describes this "springing up":

> The picture our Lord described here is not that of a simple stream of water, but an overflowing fountain. Continue to "be filled" (Ephesians 5:18) and the sweetness of your vital relationship to Jesus will flow as generously out of you as it has been given to you.[8]

I suspect that at this point the woman knew she was on to something really good but does not fully perceive the depth of Jesus's invitation until he answers her question about the Messiah. "I, the one speaking to you—I am he" (John 4:26).

Public Invitation

Jesus's public invitation to drink of the living water, from John 7:37–39, comes while he and his disciples are in Jerusalem for the Feast of Booths. This feast, occurring sometime in late September to early October, is a time of thanksgiving for the harvest. Devout Jews literally live outdoors for seven days in booths made of tree branches as a reminder of God's provision during the forty years of wilderness with Moses. Each morning, a procession travels from the temple mount to the pool of Siloam to retrieve a pitcher of water. A priest fills a gold pitcher with water and pours its contents onto the altar during the sacrifice. It is a time of celebration with trumpets blasting, great singing, and corporate rejoicing.

It is on the last day of this festival that Jesus stands and issues an astonishing invitation: "Let anyone who is thirsty come to me and drink."

The invitation is for *anyone* to come and drink. Jesus offers a totally different kind of water: *living water.* And he expands the invitation to include anyone. This is the heart of the gospel message: Jesus will quench the longing of any thirsty soul. The only prerequisite is to come and drink. He has the credentials, ability, and power to transform each thirsty soul seeking his free offer—anyone.

Jesus follows up his invitation with a requirement and a promise.

Jesus says that the living water is for "whoever believes in me." Jesus sets the criteria for this free gift—belief. This requires faith. At the heart of Jesus's invitation is his motive for coming to this earth—to seek and to save those who are lost. Christ presents himself as the living water, and anyone who comes to him will receive eternal life.

For those who believe, he then gives a promise: "Rivers of living water will flow from within them" (John 7:38–39). Once a person tastes the living water, they are forever *transformed*. This experience changes a person from the inside out.

This is the same kind of transformation Jesus offers the woman of Samaria. She receives his gift through faith and experiences the living water personally. This is living water that never dries up, never becomes stagnant, and cannot be polluted! This water is always living, and it brings a dynamic, energetic, abundant life flowing from within.

So how does this living water encounter apply to those seeking the way of worship?

First, Jesus is always the source of living water. Notice the woman's response to Jesus's invitation: "Where can you get this living water?" (John 4:11). And Jesus reveals to her that he is the Messiah. The Bible says Jesus and his disciples stayed in Samaria for two days, "and because of his words many more became believers" (John 4:40).

Second, Jesus creates within us springs of living water, a source for fresh, daily, renewable worship. This water is ever bubbling up, overflowing with blessing and spiritual nourishment. There is an endless supply. This water is always flowing out from inside each believer so that our friends, neighbors, and relatives ask the same question of us that the woman of Samaria asked Jesus: "Where can you get this living water?" Oswald Chambers says:

We are to be fountains through which Jesus can flow as "rivers of living water" in blessing to everyone. . . . As surely as we receive blessings from Him, He will pour out blessings through us. . . . Jesus says that out of you "will flow rivers of living water." It is . . . a river that continually flows through you. Stay at the Source, closely guarding your faith in Jesus Christ and your relationship to Him, and there will be a steady flow into the lives of others with no dryness or deadness whatsoever.[9]

Third, there is great satisfaction in this living water. Only Jesus can satisfy the soul. Augustine's confession aptly describes this need for Jesus: "You have made us for yourself, and our hearts are restless, until they can find rest in you."[10] The living water is life changing, refreshing to the soul, nourishing to the spirit, and eternal. The invitation is personal—it is from Jesus. The offer is for all nations—anyone may receive this living water. The response is simple—come to the fountain. The gift is freely given—come and receive:

The Spirit and the bride say, "Come!" And let the one who hears say, "Come!" Let the one who is thirsty come; and let the one who wishes take the free gift of the water of life.
—REVELATION 22:17

Once we have experienced this invitation for ourselves, we can then extend it to others in how we guide them in worship.

C. HIS POWER, OUR AWARENESS

CHAPTER 15

GENEROSITY

"You guys ever surf?" John asked us.

"Do I look like a surfer?" Neal said.

"Surfers are cute though," Franny said, smacking her gum.

"Yeah, well, they don't make surfboards that big, so I got no shot at cute, I guess. I need, like, an airplane wing or something."

Neal and Franny never lacked for one-liners.

"You guys are from Florida, right? You guys *have* to surf." John looked right at me.

"You'd think that would be the case, but I opted for basketball. Balance is not my strongest suit. Also, I'm not that cool," I replied.

"I got up on a board once, but I didn't last long, so I wouldn't call it surfing," Leah said.

"Really? Okay, we are going to surf some whitewater. It's fun. We are going to spin the raft, jump up on some whitewater, and surf a wave here in a minute."

The river narrowed, and we picked up steam as the water tumbled through the canyon. The frigid water splashed on our hot skin as we navigated the mid-level rapids.

"Okay everyone, once we cascade down that gulley, I'm going to spin us and then call forward hard, and we will paddle back upstream right up on top of that white goodness."

Down the chute we went. John quickly spun our raft using giant backward strokes.

"Forward hard!"

We dug in with all our might, and to my surprise, we were moving the raft upriver, against the current.

"Rest!" We pulled our paddles in, and we magically skated on top of the whitewater foam, facing upriver.

"Woohoo!" we all cheered. It was an exhilarating feeling riding on top of the powerful force.

After about twenty seconds, our guide paddled us off the wave, and we spun with the current and headed downriver again. We floated into some calm water, and Anastasia spoke up, which was rare for the quiet Swede.

"The river is always giving you something new, something fresh. I never get tired of it. Look at the beautiful trees, the flowers, the wildlife; it just keeps giving."

John chimed in. "Totally. The river brings life. Water is the source, man. It has given me everything. Why would I hold anything back? You can't out-give the river."

John possessed a generous spirit. He seemed bound only by the responsibility he felt to serve others. You got this sense from him during the whole trip that he would give you the shirt off his back if needed. He had great ownership of his role, but he was not owned by it—or anything, for that matter. He was free. His generosity gave us all a sense of trust in him. The counterintuitive nature of paddling upstream and surfing the foamy torrent reminded me of the against-the-culture nature that kind of generosity demonstrates.

Therefore, I urge you, brothers and sisters, in view of God's mercy, to offer your bodies as a living sacrifice, holy and pleasing to God—this is your true and proper worship.

—ROMANS 12:1

Give, and it will be given to you. A good measure, pressed down, shaken together and running over, will be poured into your lap. For with the measure you use, it will be measured to you.

—LUKE 6:38

Have you ever known or been around someone who exudes generosity? They seem ready to help, give, serve, and love in whatever way possible. They are accessible relationally and will find a way to meet a need. They bring life to situations. They provide solutions instead of complaining. They lift people up. It's so refreshing and seemingly so rare. Those who live generous lives seem so free and unencumbered from protecting what's theirs. I've heard it said that "open hands are never empty." The more we give away, the more we really have. It's a law of the universe created by God.

Generosity is counterintuitive to our human nature. If unattended, our hearts will drift toward a scarcity mentality. It's a mentality that says, "There isn't enough. I have to keep what's mine. I may run out." It's not just about money, either. It's about our posture toward God and others. We tend to grasp tightly to what we believe is ours. Our carnal nature is to be stingy—tight-fisted with our money, our time, our home, our relationships, and our words. The struggle can be stronger in one or more areas depending on a person's disposition. Some may be prone to generosity relationally but fiercely withhold their resources.

To worship fully is to understand what we've been given in Jesus:

God's mercy. In Romans 12:1, this is exactly what Paul is admonishing us to do. It's as if he is saying to us, "Look at what you've been given! Because Jesus was poured out for you, you can be poured out for him!" The original language of this passage is telling us to present the "totality of who we are" as living sacrifices of worship.

Scripture is full of the power of giving. A generous life is a blessed life. To give to others is to give to Jesus. To worship him is to be generous with him and others. We find our greatest purpose when we offer our lives back to him with all praise and thanksgiving. For anything good we have comes from him.

Our guide, John, ran the river with joy and passion. He was free to help us do the same. He wasn't owned by what he owned. May we be a people who are willing to go counter-culture and surf the whitewater of hilarious giving, and worship our Savior more fully.

Now we come to the halfway point of our journey together. This is an exciting moment—not a stopping place, but a time to rest and redirect our focus to one of preparation. We now have the tools needed to discover and establish a plan of action in our own personal worship. These principles afford balance (with added perspective) as we move forward in our study and enable us to find ways to better serve the Lord and one another.

Generosity is an important first step of any preparation for worship. It involves a quality of life that is both a testimony of a person's character and a reflection of a deep commitment to worship. James 1:17 reads, "Every good and perfect gift is from [God]." Of course, a person can be generous (and even give freely) and never worship, but a person actively engaged in worship of Jesus out of a contrite and broken spirit will always give with a heart of generosity as unto the Lord.

The Old Testament prophet Isaiah reminds us that "a generous man devises generous things, and by generosity he shall stand" (Isa 32:8 NKJV). Generosity is an act of the will. While every good and perfect gift comes from God to us as his children, our willingness to share these gifts with others gives evidence of our surrender to the Lord. Each worshiper must purposefully and faithfully practice living a spirit of generosity, which is then nurtured by the working of the Holy Spirit in our heart.

If you recall, we studied briefly about worship through giving in chapter 10. In that study, we discovered that one of the important ingredients in biblical worship involves "giving to the Lord." Psalm 96:7–8 encourages us to give to the Lord glory and strength. And only after we acknowledge his goodness with our worship do we bring an offering into his courts. A person that is faithful to worship in spirit and truth naturally demonstrates adoration to the Lord with a generous and unselfish spirit.

Generosity is the quality of being kind and generous.[1] It implies a "readiness to give" and a "freedom from meanness or smallness of mind or character."[2] Generosity—like honesty, patience, unselfishness, hospitality, or kindness—demonstrates willingness to serve and give to others free from agenda or motive. It involves seeing and responding to the needs of others with a spirit of grace and love.

So how does a person seeking to prepare themselves for the way of worship develop this spirit of generosity in their lives?

We must generously surrender *everything* to the Lord. Surrendering our attitude or spirit of generosity reflects a worshiper's commitment to yield personal ambitions, motives, goals, and even opportunities to the Lord. Surrender is an attitude of heart that prompts the worshiper to *willingly give up ownership*. This primarily involves being gracious and generous with the things that people never see—it is a heart attitude. St. Francis of Assisi reminds us that "it is in giving that we receive."[3] So how do these attitudes give evidence of generosity in a person's life?

There are many aspects of our lives where the Holy Spirit teaches us to be generous.

1. Generous with our words. "One person gives freely, yet gains even more; another withholds unduly, but comes to poverty. A generous person will prosper; whoever refreshes others will be refreshed" (Prov 11:24–25; emphasis added).

2. Generous with our wisdom. As the Holy Spirit teaches us wisdom, understanding, and knowledge (Prov 3:19–20), we learn to give to others freely, graciously, and lovingly.

3. Generous in our conduct. "Whoever is kind to the poor lends to the LORD, and he will reward them for what they have done" (Prov 19:17).

4. Generous in our motives. "For where your treasure is, there your heart will be also" (Matt 6:21). This includes graciously giving out of a willing spirit our knowledge, love, understanding, and emotions. "Each of you should give what you have decided in your heart to give, not reluctantly or under compulsion, for God loves a cheerful giver" (2 Cor 9:7).

5. Generous with ourselves. "Do not forget to show hospitality to strangers, for by so doing some people have shown hospitality to angels without knowing it." (Heb 13:2). "And do not forget to do good and to share with others, for with such sacrifices God is pleased" (Heb 13:16). For the worshiper, this includes our time, talent, counsel, and personal commitment to meet the needs of others.

Fred Rogers once said, "The greatest gift you ever give is your honest self."[4] We must generously submit everything to the Lord. While surrender is an attitude, submission is an action. It is generously carrying out in word and deed the heart attitude of surrender. This involves being gracious and generous with our stuff. Submission to the spirit of generosity means the worshiper graciously and gracefully gives unto the Lord.

6. Generous with our substance. "Remember this: Whoever sows sparingly will also reap sparingly, and whoever sows generously will also reap generously" (2 Cor 9:6). This includes our money, our possessions, our wealth, our belongings—our stuff!

7. Generous with our strength. "Do not withhold good from those to whom it is due; when it is in your power to act. Do not say to your neighbor, 'Come back tomorrow and I'll give it to you'" (Prov 3:27–28). "Give to the LORD, O families of the peoples, Give to the LORD glory and strength" (Ps 96:7 NKJV). This involves our expertise, skill, labor, physical effort, exercise . . . everything.

8. Generous with our service. "If you spend yourselves in behalf of the hungry and satisfy the needs of the oppressed, then your light will rise in the darkness, and your night will become like the noonday. The LORD will guide you always; he will satisfy your needs in a sunscorched land and will strengthen your frame. You will be like a wellwatered garden, like a spring whose waters never fail" (Isa 58:10–11). This involves working, serving, and giving of our talent and craft.

9. Generous with our sacrifice. "One person gives freely, yet gains even more; another withholds unduly, but comes to poverty" (Prov 11:24). "But [David] replied to Araunah, 'No, I insist on paying you for it. I will not sacrifice to the LORD my God burnt offerings that cost me nothing.' . . . David built an altar to the LORD there and sacrificed burnt offerings and fellowship offerings. Then the LORD answered his prayer in behalf of the land" (2 Sam 24:24–25). In principle, we should ask ourselves whether our sacrifice of worship is genuine if it doesn't really cost us anything.

Generosity begins with an attitude and is consummated with an action. The Bible specifically requires those who name the name of Jesus to be generous with their treasure and good stewards of their time. The Holy Spirit enables us to be victorious over the sins of greed and selfishness. And in the words of Winston Churchill, "We make a living by what we get, but we make a life by what we give."[5] As we learn the joy of generosity, perhaps we should be faithful to remember the four types of biblical gifts.

First, there are gifts of humility, or alms. The Bible categorizes gifts to the poor as "alms." The spirit of this kind of giving has everything to do with being generous and gracious to the marginalized and less fortunate. Gifts falling into this category may include shelter, food, clothing, and monetary assistance.

Second, there are gifts of honesty, or tithes. The prophet Malachi follows the precedent set by the book of Leviticus when he asks about tithing:

> "Will a mere mortal rob God? Yet you rob me.
>
> "But you ask, 'How are we robbing you?'
>
> "In tithes and offerings. You are under a curse—your whole nation—because you are robbing me. Bring the whole tithe into the storehouse, that there may be food in my house. Test me in this," says the Lord Almighty, "and see if I will not throw open the floodgates of heaven and pour out so much blessing that there will not be room enough to store it."
>
> —MALACHI 3:8–10

In more recent years, some have argued that "the tithe" is an Old Testament practice not to be observed by those redeemed by grace. They argue that although there are biblical examples of tithing in Abraham, Moses, and Jesus, we have the freedom in Christ not to give a tithe. In reality, everything we own belongs to God, and he allows us to steward his blessings. And it is our privilege and honor to give back to God 10 percent (the tithe) willingly, not grudgingly and unto the Lord. And our worship is deeper and richer as we learn the joy of giving unto the Lord a portion of the substance with which God has blessed us.[6]

Third, there are honorable gifts, or offerings. This includes free-will offerings and the gift of "firstfruits" (Prov 3:9–10; Neh 10:30). There are thirty-one references in the Bible to firstfruits. These gifts are given as an expression of God's blessings for all he has done and is doing. To the farmer, it includes harvest in grain, fruit, or any other form of "first income" for the year.[7]

And finally, there are helping gifts, or gifts of grace. These are gifts above and beyond what God expects. This is when a person has the ability to give beyond the "normal" tithes and offerings. In many ways, these are gifts without limit from the hearts of grateful people—most often given anonymously.[8]

CHAPTER 16

EQUIPPING

"How's that vest fitting?" Before we launched the raft that morning, Anastasia checked our gear. She grabbed the front of my vest and yanked. I was surprised by the strength of the small Swedish apprentice.

"It's too loose. We can't have dat."

She reached around my ribcage and jerked the straps tight until they wouldn't pull any farther. She pulled on the front of my vest again. Her proximity made me uncomfortable.

"Am I supposed to be able to breathe?" I asked.

"You're fine."

"Ana! How's the checklist?" John barked out as he tied the cooler down in the raft.

"All set!"

"PFDs?"

"Check."

"Brain buckets?"

"Check."

"First aid?"

"Check."

"Rescue throw bag?"

She paused, looking though the raft. No sign of it. She raced over to the van and pulled it out of the back. "Throw bag, check!"

John watched her with eyebrows raised as she walked back to the raft and put the throw bag in. "Looks like that box wasn't checked."

Anastasia stayed quiet.

As the team was getting the last of the gear loaded into the raft, I went back to the van to grab some gum from my backpack, and Anastasia was shutting the back doors.

"Did you get in trouble?" I asked, half joking.

"Not really." She grinned as she continued, "He is just looking out for us. He wants to make sure we are ready when it is our time to guide. The stakes are high out here, so I welcome the instruction. I don't want anyone to get hurt."

"That must be intense, having him always checking up on you, looking over your shoulder," I said.

"I guess. I look at it more like a guardian angel. Well, an angel that tells me what to do." She chuckled.

"He's the best teacher, really. He is passing on what he learned from his father. It really helps me feel prepared and more confident. It doesn't bother me, really. I need it. I don't want to make a grave mistake."

Her demeanor seemed humble toward John and reverent toward the task at hand.

"So does he just instruct as you go, or do you have classes or something?"

"All of it. I take courses in water safety, first aid, and hydrology. I take guide training courses. He meets with apprentice guides weekly. We have certifications and tests we have to go through. We also have a briefing before every trip. We actually met for an hour before you came in this morning. We will meet after to evaluate how it went and what we can learn. We are constantly learning. The more you know, the more confident you become. John always says, 'It's the way of the guide.'"

I found that whatever nerves I had were waning, and my comfort grew in knowing the lengths to which these guides go to stay ready, equipping themselves and each other for the great privilege and responsibility of guiding.

And He Himself gave some to be apostles, some prophets, some evangelists, and some pastors and teachers, for the *equipping* of the saints for the work of ministry, for the *edifying* of the body of Christ, till we all come to the unity of the faith and of the knowledge of the Son of God, to a perfect man, to the measure of the stature of the fullness of Christ.

—EPHESIANS 4:11–13; EMPHASIS ADDED

To be equipped and to equip others is essential for every guide. John was not only a voracious learner, hungry for the knowledge and wisdom of the river, but he was a passionate equipper. To be equipped, we must possess a humility and a hunger to learn. We must chase after wisdom with all our might. John knew that for the success of every rafting trip, and therefore the success of their company, they had to equip their apprentices for the task at hand. It was not enough to just say, "Take a raft and head down the river!" That would be disastrous and make for a very short-lived rafting company. Every guide had to humble themselves into learning the language, the gear, the techniques, the people skills, the watershed, the fitness, the first aid, and on and on. Learning had to be a way of life. It was not enough to learn for yourself, either; they would also pass along their expertise and knowledge to others as they grew in their ability and experience.

It was the way of the guide. It was about passion, calling, and a sacred stewardship.

> The one who gets wisdom loves life;
> the one who cherishes understanding will soon prosper.
> —PROVERBS 19:8

As worship leaders, or "guides," we are engaging in a beautiful, dangerous, and mysterious journey. As we ourselves are being equipped, we are deepening our knowledge of and passion for the river of life. We are learning about the safety equipment—the armor of God. We are tuning our spiritual ears to the sound of the river's voice as we meditate on God's Word and spend time in deep prayer. We are discovering the dangerous and sinful obstacles that want to trap us. We are becoming great river runners—river runners that know and are known by "the waters." We are apprentices being led by great mentors, teachers, pastors, and masters of the craft. We are on the journey to becoming master guides in helping people encounter and worship the river of life, Jesus. To be equipped and equip others is the pursuit of every guide in training.

We must stay in a posture of humble learning. For it is in this chasing of wisdom that our lives and the lives of others will be spared from undue, self-inflicted disaster.

> Wisdom's instruction is to fear the LORD,
> and humility comes before honor.
> —PROVERBS 15:33

> A proud man is always looking down on things and people; and, of course, as long as you are looking down, you cannot see something that is above you.
> —C. S. LEWIS

Being equipped and knowing how to equip others is critically important to the role of worship leader. This is preparation for the mission God calls us to as worshipers.

The worshiper responsible for *doing the equipping* actually supplies necessities—such as tools, materials, provisions, services, or ability—to accomplish the mission. This involves provision of needed materials to fulfill the mission to which we've been called to as worshipers.

Those committed to the way of worship should understand that what we do is reproducible. At the end of the day, our goal is to promote and bring into the body of Christ (the church) citizens from every tribe, tongue, culture, nation, or people group. Why? So that they can become worshipers too!

> My son, be strong in the grace that is in Christ Jesus. And the things you have heard me say in the presence of many witnesses entrust to reliable people who will also be qualified to teach others. Join with me in suffering, like a good soldier of Christ Jesus.
> —2 TIMOTHY 2:1–3

We have been commanded to go into all the world and make fully devoted followers of Christ—worshipers. This is putting feet on the formational, transformational, relational, and missional aspects of worship. When we are either being equipped or involved in the process of equipping, we are participating in a part of the Christian mission called discipleship! This is preparation in action.

There is a huge difference between being a teacher and an equipper (or disciple-maker). Teaching involves giving instruction, providing information, and imparting knowledge. A teacher does not necessarily take on the role of equipping. But to the worshiper-trainer, equipping always involves some level of teaching, tutoring, mentoring, developing, and nurturing new worshiping disciples. It involves coming alongside others in a personal capacity.

We become part of the transformation process itself each time we take on the role of equipping as we teach, train, develop, and nurture new worshipers. Contextualization becomes reality. We relate our message and mission to the culture in which God strategically places us to serve. We live out in our daily routine, or lifestyle evangelism, the task of equipping in personal and private worship. We communicate the Word of God by the way we live. Each time we engage in leading biblical worship, we help pass the understanding of and ability to worship on to others.

There are both personal and professional aspects to being equipped and equipping others for service in worship.

Personal Equipping

Being equipped is a deeply personal and private matter because it deals with issues of the heart. This kind of equipping drills down to the core of one's being. The writer of Hebrews puts it this way:

> Now may the God of peace, who through the blood of the eternal covenant brought back from the dead our Lord Jesus, that great Shepherd of the sheep, *equip you with everything good for doing his will*, and may he work in us what is pleasing to him, through Jesus Christ, to whom be glory for ever and ever. Amen.
> —HEBREWS 13:20–21; EMPHASIS ADDED

Notice here that the actual process of "being equipped" is accomplished through the working of the Holy Spirit in the life of the worshiper. The Holy Spirit equips us with everything we need *to do his will*. This is God's sovereignty at work: he equips us. And the worshiper's response is obedience—doing his will. This working of the Holy Spirit is deeply personal and regulated by God's Word in Scripture.

The original Greek word for equip means "to fit or join together, mend or repair"—putting something into its appropriate condition so it will function well.[1] Literally, it means to be complete, fully trained, mended, perfectly prepared, or restored.[2]

In modern Greek, the word is used as a medical term for when a physician sets a broken bone. Charles Spurgeon, the great English preacher, applies this to the fall of Adam in "the garden":

> By the [sinful] fall, all our bones are out of joint for the doing of the Lord's will. The desire of the apostle is that the Lord will set the bones in their places, and thus make us able with every faculty and in every good work to do His will.[3]

For worshipers, equipping means setting right what has gone wrong, or restoring to a former condition. We must thoroughly prepare worshipers to meet the demands of God's call in leading men, women, boys, and girls to worship. Much like when a physician sets a broken bone, God "mends our broken lives and makes us fully whole"[4] so that we can serve him and more completely fulfill his purposes in our lives. The practical application involves equipping worshipers so that they are sufficiently and adequately trained for the task at hand.

The Bible outlines a clear process for being equipped in 2 Timothy:

> All Scripture is God-breathed and is useful for teaching, rebuking, correcting and training in righteousness, so that the servant of God may be *thoroughly equipped* for every good work.
> —2 TIMOTHY 3:16–17; EMPHASIS ADDED

The process of equipping for worship can be broken down into four questions and answers:

1. What is God doing? Thoroughly equipping the worshiper.
2. How does God equip? Worshipers are continually being equipped by the Word of God.
3. Who is being equipped? Worship leaders, individuals—men and women obeying the call to lead worship.
4. What are they equipped for? Worshipers are being equipped to do every good work.

In the final analysis, the Holy Spirit works in us as we read, understand, and live the truth (Scripture) more clearly. The Holy Spirit uses our own life experiences, opportunities, relationships, and learning moments—whatever is pleasing to him—to help equip us to see, know, worship, and follow Jesus more perfectly. Why? So that he can receive glory, honor, and praise (Heb 13:21b).

We have spent much of this book looking into the issues of the heart, where God equips us for worship by making us more like Christ in our inward persons and willful behavior. But there is another aspect to preparing people to lead worship, and that is our public and professional life.

Professional Equipping

Equipping someone professionally means helping them fill in the gaps so they can better fulfill a particular task or purpose. In our story, the river guide diligently goes through a checklist to make sure all supplies and tools are available for the rafting journey. Every item is accounted for and inventoried. The river guide gives those in the raft (and those coming behind) all the training, resources, and encouragement they need to navigate the journey.

This is similar to the kind of equipping the apostle Paul is referring to when defining the various positions necessary for ministry:

So Christ himself gave the apostles, the prophets, the evangelists, the pastors and teachers, to equip his people for works of service, so

that the body of Christ may be built up until we all reach unity in the faith and in the knowledge of the Son of God and become mature, attaining to the whole measure of the fullness of Christ.
—EPHESIANS 4:11–13; EMPHASIS ADDED

It is curious to me that this word, *equipping*, first appears in the New Testament at the time Jesus calls Peter, Andrew, James, and John to be his disciples. Jesus is walking along the Sea of Galilee and sees the four fishermen sitting in a boat, "mending their nets." This word "mending" is the same Greek word for equip or equipping (*katartizo*). These brothers are "equipping their nets," making them strong for service, and getting them ready for their next day's work![5]

Ray Stedman suggests that in the original Greek the word for equipping is the very same source from which we get our English word *artisan*. Artisans are craftsmen that work with their hands to make or build things.[6] It is this unique "artisan" role worshipers assume when given the task of building and equipping.

Worship leaders develop their craft better each time they lead worship. They build their confidence each time they equip people for works of service. They strengthen character every time they reach unity in the faith. They lead worship as a calling so that the body of Christ may be built up in the knowledge of the Son of God.

Like the water rafters gathering supplies for their river expedition or the disciples mending their broken fish nets for their next day's labor, we need to be equipped for the journey as leaders of worship. The equipping worshipers receive is especially administered by the Holy Spirit. It is necessary for several reasons.

It is necessary to *supply wisdom and strength* for facing the positive and negative forces created by the storyline culture writes upon our life.

The Holy Spirit equips us in order to enlighten the worshiper's mind *to understand the Word of God*, which provides a *deeper awareness of God's call* to lead.

It is necessary to *provide unity of faith* so worshipers grow *to the measure of the stature of the fullness of Christ within the community* in which they live and serve, influencing their families, friendships, workplace relationships, and faith-based environments.

Equipping is necessary to *encourage and cultivate* daily *communion with God,* ensuring a deeper relationship with the Lord we worship.

Equipping strengthens us to *overcome conflict* and misunderstanding *with those traveling along with us* on this worship journey.

And finally, the Holy Spirit inspires us to *seize upon commonplace,* every day, run-of-the-mill—when nobody is looking—*activities that help shape our character* and reveal our integrity to others.

CHAPTER 17

EMPOWERING

"The sidewinder is all you, Ana!"

Ana looked bewildered.

"You know what to do," John said encouragingly. "Let's switch. You take the command on this rapid."

John and Anastasia gripped forearms as they stood and swapped places. John moved to the port side rear, and Ana moved to the guide's perch at the center on the back tube.

"Everyone please take your commands from the Swede on this next rapid. It's a tricky one . . . very technical," John said.

I looked back to see Ana secure her foot under the side tube and give the strap on her PFD a tug to make sure it was tight enough. She had joy on her face and focus in her eyes.

"Remember what we discussed?" John asked her directly.

She nodded. "Then tell me."

"Enter first rapid from the right, clear boulder one, forward hard then left forward hard to boulder two, then rest briefly, two pulls backward left side then straight ahead forward hard into final drop."

"Excellent. And what do we always remember?"

"Trust the plan, adapt if necessary?"

"Good work, but that's not a question. It's a statement." John smiled kindly through his instruction. I was struck by his clear and measured tone.

He did not coddle, nor did he demean. I was a first-timer, but his forthrightness gave me a level of confidence in his ability, Ana's ability, and my own. I never felt the sense that he was instructing from a need for power or authority, only service and purpose. His presence and manner were impressive in all the right ways.

The river picked up speed, and the rumbling whitewater ushered us into the next rapid. Ana began calling her commands.

"Left forward hard!" Our raft pointed starboard.

"Left rest, right forward hard!" We turned back into the rapid toward a large boulder. We cascaded down and up, splashing through the spray of the frigid flow. Shouts and laughter ensued as we were having a wonderful time.

"Left." John said calmly. Then he shouted it twice much louder. "Left, left!"

He stuck his paddle in the water on the port side and steered our raft. We swooshed over a boulder barely sticking out of the water. I felt it hit my foot as we got hung up.

"Forward hard! Forward hard!" both guides yelled. We pulled ourselves off the rock, but bumping the rock spun our raft, and immediately we were backward, heading into the next drop.

"Backward hard!" We careened over the next rapid in reverse, and then John strained and dug deep into the water with his paddle, quickly spinning us around after we navigated safely.

"I'm sorry, I'm sorry. I missed that call." Ana looked dejected.

"We made it and avoided an unnecessary brisk swim, thankfully."

"It happened so quickly, I just missed it."

"It's okay, you learned what not to do next time. That's why I'm here. It happens. Move forward. You can do this."

These things command and teach. Let no one despise your youth, but
be an example to the believers in word, in conduct, in love, in spirit,
in faith, in purity. Till I come, give attention to reading, to exhortation,
to doctrine. Do not neglect the gift that is in you, which was given
to you by prophecy with the laying on of the hands of the eldership.

—1 TIMOTHY 4:11–14

Empowering others effectively means giving them power or confidence, and it requires humility. It requires a secure identity for the
leader who is empowering. Many leaders tend to control, meddle, or
micromanage because they have not effectively equipped those under
them or are threatened by the loss of power. But in order for others
to grow, it is essential that leaders empower them to make decisions,
execute those decisions, and learn from them.

I (Michael) have three children. At every stage I have to teach them
and equip them with the skills they need to make decisions. But then
I need to let them actually make the decision. I've watched my wife
teach our kids to cook. She shows them the temperature of the stove,
how to handle the utensils with care, the proper ingredients to use,
and how to tend the meal. Little by little, she relinquishes each task to
them until they are ready to prepare the meal on their own. It's a thing
of beauty to behold. It's what I call "supportive empowerment." She's
there, ready to help, guide, and serve until one day, they will be ready
to make it on their own. If we do this well and our children remain
hungry to learn, we will hopefully set them up for a strong life of good
decision making.

Our guide, John, embodied supportive empowerment. I watched
him equip his apprentice with the necessary training, but he didn't
stop there. He allowed her to lead while he was still in the raft. He
knew she wasn't fully ready to take on the responsibility of a full raft

of people by herself, but he supported her to begin the process and was there to pull her out of a jam when she made a mistake.

As we grow in our leadership of others in pursuit of the way of worship, we must learn the principle of empowerment. Empowering others to lead, guide, and make decisions in our worship ministries is vital to our call to disciple others. Empowering others does not mean we don't get to lead in our gifting. It just means we recognize it's not about us, and the greater purpose is to multiply our efforts for the mission. Our mission is to help as many people as possible find their life and purpose in surrendered worship of Jesus, the river of life. That cannot happen without us becoming supportive leaders who give away power and confidence to those we lead.

> Most people think leadership is about being in charge. Most people think leadership is about having all the answers and being the most intelligent person or the most qualified person in the room. The irony is that it is the complete opposite. Leadership is about empowering others to achieve things they did not think possible. Leadership is about pointing in the direction, articulating a vision of the world that does not yet exist. Then asking help from others to ensure that vision happens.
>
> —SIMON SINEK

In our last chapter, we discovered that we must both be equipped and equip others as worshipers. We are to be equipped through personal training, individual preparation, and perfecting for the mission God calls one to as a worshiper. We equip others by taking the time to gather necessities and supplies—such as tools, materials, provisions, or services—to accomplish the mission.

Similarly, empowering is something that we must both experience and do for others. Being empowered is personal. Empowerment means making someone (in our case, worshipers) strong, more confident, self-assured, and certain.[1] As we are empowered, we engage in a process of development. Jesus implies this process when he tells the disciples,

> But you will receive power [being empowered] when the Holy Spirit comes on you; and you will be my witnesses in Jerusalem, and in all Judea and Samaria, and to the ends of the earth.
>
> —ACTS 1:8

Empowering others, on the other hand, means giving them the authority or permission to do something. It is a type of authorization, license, or certification.[2] Just as John (in the story above) gave Ana the authority to direct the rafters, Jesus grants authority when he refers to the empowering process:

> Then Jesus came to them and said, "All authority in heaven and on earth has been given to me. Therefore go and make disciples of all nations, baptizing them in the name of the Father and of the Son and of the Holy Spirit, and teaching them to obey everything I have commanded you. And surely I am with you always, to the very end of the age."
>
> —MATTHEW 28:18–20

Empower is a transitive verb, meaning it shows action, but it must also have an object to which the action is applied. Someone must receive the empowering. The worshiper is being empowered, trained, fortified, or strengthened for the task of leading. Church leaders empower by giving authority or permission for worshipers to lead the congregational time of praise. We empower others by delegating work to them, letting them learn the skills to become leaders themselves. We teach principles of mentoring. Then we empower them to mentor others.

Two passages of Scripture demonstrate how God uniquely empowers his people with strength and authority to do a task.

The first is found in Luke 9:1–6, when Jesus sends out his disciples to preach the gospel, heal the sick, and cast out evil spirits:

> When Jesus had called the Twelve together, he gave them *power and authority* to drive out all demons and to cure diseases, and he sent them out to proclaim the kingdom of God and to heal the sick. . . . So they set out and went from village to village, proclaiming the good news and healing people everywhere.
>
> —LUKE 9:1–2, 6

Notice that Jesus *provides* for these disciples the strength, equipping, ability, and miraculous power to do the task. The word for power is from the Greek (*dunamis*) that gives us the English word for *dynamite*.[3]

Jesus gives the disciples *authority*. So Jesus empowers his disciples and gives them the authority, or the proper credentials, to see the task through.

The second example is in the Old Testament. God empowers a man named Bezalel with wisdom and skill for the task of crafting the ornaments and tools for worship in the tabernacle, where God's people will worship while wandering in the desert.[4]

> Then Moses said to the Israelites, "See, the Lord has chosen Bezalel . . . and he has filled him with the Spirit of God, with wisdom, with understanding, with knowledge and with all kinds of skills. . . . And he has given both him and Oholiab son of Ahisamak, of the tribe of Dan, the ability to teach others. . . . He has filled [Bezalel] with skill to do all kinds of work."
>
> —EXODUS 35:30–35

Bezalel is a master workman under the command of Moses. God empowers Bezalel both to carry out the task and to teach others how to do the work with him. He has the authority to replicate the skills in the lives of other workmen and artisans.

God empowers Bezalel with multiple gifts of workmanship to design artistic works; work in gold, silver, and bronze; cut jewels for setting; carve wood, create cloth, make tapestry, scarlet thread, and fine linen; function as a fashion designer; and do all manner of artistic workmanship. Then God calls this multitalented Bezalel into action, empowering him to supervise all those that will come alongside of him and assist him in the tasks.

Note the juxtaposition of God's sovereign work and human obedience, which is an outgrowth of God's empowering. God does all the strengthening, fortifying, and empowering in the worshiper. And the worshiper does the work through the empowering of the Holy Spirit indwelling in him or her—obedience.

Why are these two examples important to the way of worship? Both demonstrate the process God uses to empower those he calls to service. Jesus "called his twelve disciples together" in Luke 9. God called Bezalel by name. And just like the disciples and Bezalel obeyed when called, God is looking for worshipers to obey, with their own gifts, when called.

Supportive empowerment is a key element of being a worship leader. Michael's wife (in the metaphor above), when helping their children learn how to cook, is ready to help, guide, and serve until one day, they will be ready to make it on their own. This kind of supportive empowerment is exactly what God provides when he grants power and authority to do that which he calls you and me to do.

I pray that from his glorious, unlimited resources he will empower you with inner strength through his Spirit.
—EPHESIANS 3:16 NLT

I can do all things [which He has called me to do] through Him who strengthens and empowers me [to fulfill His purpose—I am self-sufficient in Christ's sufficiency; I am ready for anything and equal to anything through Him who infuses me with inner strength and confident peace.]

—PHILIPPIANS 4:13 AMPLIFIED BIBLE

God wants to empower, strengthen, equip, and make you ready for action to lead others in worship. God has uniquely gifted you, and he wants you to use your gifts and skillset for the purpose of advancing his kingdom. He empowers and equips through the power of his Holy Spirit living in you.

Those seeking the way of worship need to remember that they have a dual role when being obedient to the call to lead worship. *First, they need to be empowered by the work of the Holy Spirit in their lives. Second, they need to empower others to lead worship,* rather than holding onto the power and authority themselves. Just as worshipers are equipped for service, they need to be busy equipping others to serve alongside them.

God is ultimately the one that prepares us for the task of leading worship, including the ability to train, equip, and empower others. Let's remember that when God calls us to serve, he *promises* to equip and empower us. And when he obligates himself to equip—whether by formal education or through the school of hard knocks and real-life experience—he obligates himself to provide in every area. When he obligates himself to empower, God obligates himself to perfect (equip), establish, strengthen (empower), and settle a person's work and ministry—for his glory and for the testimony of Jesus Christ (1 Pet 5:10–11).

CHAPTER 18

UNIFYING

"When's our next break? I'm tired, and I have a headache. It's pounding me like a hammah," Franny moaned in her thick Brooklyn accent.

"It's only been thirty minutes, princess!" Neal responded to his wife with some frustration. These two went at each other constantly.

Neal backhanded me on the shoulder, almost knocking me out of the boat. "It's always somethin'," he said under his breath. Neal jeered in a gruff falsetto voice as if to imitate her, tilting his head back and forth with every descriptor. "She's too cold, she's too hot, she's tired, she's hungry, she stubbed her toe, she chipped a nail. I can't take it."

"Oh, *you* can't take it? *You* can't take it?" Franny asked, nodding her head. "Who snores so loud it's like Amtrak chugging through my room?" She gestured like she was pulling the train horn. "Who's always downing Tums like candy, whining about his little heartburn? Huh? Huh?"

Neal shrugged his shoulders and looked at me. "I don't know what she's talking about."

"You listen here, buddy boy. You're lucky I put up with *you*."

"Yes, sweet pea, we are both very lucky." Neal rolled his eyes.

"Don't you . . . " Franny pointed her finger but got interrupted by John.

"Friends, friends, it's a beautiful day!" the guide chuckled. "Okay, before we start navigating some bigger water, let's talk paddling technique."

We floated gently through the expansive gorge. The sun wasn't fully above the canyon walls yet, and a quiet chill blanketed the atmosphere.

"One hand on the T-grip, one hand on the shaft halfway down. Be sure to engage your entire paddle in the water, not just the tip. It's counterintuitive, but the river actually stabilizes you when your paddle is fully engaged. That's what will keep you in the boat in the big water. If you skim the surface, you'll be swimming before you know it." John demonstrated the technique for us. When he took a stroke, you could feel the raft lunge forward. "When you paddle, you gotta mean it. It's important that we all dig in and execute powerfully together. If I give a 'forward hard' command and one side doesn't dig in, what do you think happens?"

"We spin?" I replied quickly.

"Yes, and if we spin and head sideways into a deep rapid or some falls, what happens?"

"We swim," Leah replied.

"Exactly. We spin, we swim. Unity is everything, so let's work together so that everyone experiences something spectacular . . . and we all stay safe."

How good and pleasant it is
    when God's people live together in unity!
It is like precious oil poured on the head,
    running down on the beard,

running down on Aaron's beard,
down on the collar of his robe.
It is as if the dew of Hermon
were falling on Mount Zion.
For there the LORD bestows his blessing,
even life forevermore.

—PSALM 133

When a unit, team, or group is unified, powerful things happen. Goals are reached. Relationships thrive. The enemy is conquered. The team wins. The family is peaceful. The rafters will experience the river safely and enjoy its power and beauty only when they paddle together. Unity is the foundation for strength, effectiveness, and beauty in life. It's how the maker designed it: unity with God, unity with others. The way of worship calls us into relationship with the unified triune God, his purposes, and his will for us all. From that relationship springs our pursuit of unity with one another.

On the other hand, when there is division and discord, everything is weakened and ineffectual. Division causes confusion and disarray, and will ultimately lead to disaster. Think of an orchestra where the instrumentalists do not follow the notations in the music or the conductor's unifying baton. What would that sound like? Chaos. No music would be made. When all submit to the will of the music and the conductor, transcendent beauty fills the air as a result of that unity.

John, the guide, was very intentional about keeping the rafters unified so that they had the safest and most exciting trip possible. He created an atmosphere where the rafters could direct their attention to the river and desire to see more. He made it fun, not a chore. He pointed the rafters to the reward of being a unified group. He knew what dangers and joys lay ahead.

This is what a great guide does. He casts a vision for the ultimate good and then trains and leads toward that good. If he didn't say it or describe it, and if he didn't demonstrate in the calm water, we would not understand it in the dangerous torrent. As John C. Maxwell said, "We're either preparing or repairing." We should never mistake *unity* with *uniformity*. Each worshiper is unique. God did not create us to look the same, feel the same, or have the same gifts, influence, or experience. He created us each unique. It is when these *parts* of the same *body* come together in harmony that beauty and order, relationship and peace, love and connection ensue.

Groups won't just drift toward excellence or unity. It takes effort. It takes intentionality. We must work against pride and self-aggrandizement. We must fight for unity. When everyone wants to go their own way, when people try to divide the team because of their own woundedness or insecurity, we must lead toward a higher and better way. We must point to unity and hold it high as the only way. As a leader of worshipers and teams of musicians, artists, technicians, and leaders, this has to be at the fore of our culture creation. Without unity we will be a rudderless raft, a conductorless and chaotic orchestra, a leaderless army that will destroy itself with friendly fire. Remember, as we lead ourselves, our families, and our teams, if we are not a unified *raft of paddlers*, we will spin. In the dangerous rapids of life, "if we spin, we swim."

In our last chapter, we discovered the "dual role" of *being empowered* and *empowering* as worshipers. Now we draw attention to a key element in that empowering process—unifying. Learning how to lead a group toward unity is a key aspect of understanding how to follow the way of worship.

The task of unifying cannot happen in the life of a worshiper without first developing a spirit of generosity, being equipped by the Holy Spirit, and learning how to empower others. Nor can a unifying spirit be demonstrated without the worshiper's commitment to serving, sacrificing, and giving.

Evidence of a Unified Team

Unity is the "state of being joined together."[1] Unity is a central principle in many spheres of life and study, from mathematics to poetry, drama to law, music to science, and beyond. This is especially true of any discipline or area of life that relies on groups of people working together, like government, the military, education, musical ensembles, praise teams, and hundreds of other areas. There is an entire academic discipline focused on understanding unity. Unity is critical to the success of most everything in life.

This is no less true for those following the way of worship. As we saw in the story and metaphor above, unity is foundational to joy as a group: "How good and pleasant it is when God's people live together in unity!" (Ps 133:1). When a worship team or a Christian group is unified, they dwell together in "oneness of mind, sentiment, affection and behavior."[2] There are clear benefits to the entire team. So what are the evidences of a spirit of unity for the worshiper?

A Team Is Forged

Unity is foundational to building a team, and helps it operate as a single unit instead of many competing individuals. It is amazing how the Holy Spirit prompts a team when there is unity among likeminded members. Ecclesiastes offers insight into the advantages of this type of collaboration:

> Two are better than one,
>> because they have a good return for their labor:
> If either of them falls down,
>> one can help the other up.
> But pity anyone who falls
>> and has no one to help them up.
>
> —ECCLESIASTES 4:9–10

Individuals double their strength when working on a team. They get more done, reap the value of having successfully worked on a project in tandem with others, and find satisfaction and joy in the fellowship of others of like mind and heart. As one writer says, "They find value in working in unison, thus creating harmony instead of disorder."[3]

Divisions Cease

The Bible teaches that believers are to be "perfectly united in mind and thought." In giving instruction to the believers at Corinth, Paul writes,

> I appeal to you, brothers and sisters, in the name of our Lord Jesus Christ, that all of you agree with one another in what you say and that there be no divisions among you, but that you be perfectly united in mind and thought.
>
> —1 CORINTHIANS 1:10

This scriptural admonition recognizes membership in one body: the church. Individually, we may feel like we are all alone, but we are not. We are part of a wonderful, worshiping community. As worshipers, it is important to remember that Christ's gift of salvation is available to each person alike. Jesus died, rose from the grave, and lives today so that every man, woman, boy, and girl can become a worshiper. His gift of salvation provides eternal life for all who believe. It is the same Holy Spirit that miraculously dwells in the heart of all naming the name of Jesus. And this same Jesus provides and nurtures in the worshiper a spirit of unity. He binds us together as his body like a family.

The entire team is at their strongest when they are one in heart, mind, and purpose. They reach goals more efficiently. The mission is clarified, and they are able to establish vision. Then the team begins to demonstrate and articulate a set of values. It is in this environment that relationships thrive, worshiping communities grow, and the family of God is ultimately at peace. Unified teamwork is the key to success and in the process, Satan is defeated, the unity of the Spirit is preserved (Eph 4:1-4), and the body of Christ can focus on equipping worshipers for doing the will of God.

How to Create a Unified Team

Unity comes from the Greek word *henótēs*, meaning "unanimity." It describes a spirit of oneness, being in harmony, or relating to others in one accord. This form of unity is not merely external but an internal, spiritual bonding together.

There are four strategic ingredients for the creation of a unified team: unity of one mind, unity of heart, unity of love, and unity of spirit.

1. Unity of one mind. Cultivating a unity of mind requires casting aside self-centeredness. The leader must have a spirit of humility, give preference to others, and follow the example of Christ. Philippians 2:3-5 says those seeking to be unified must "Do nothing out of selfish ambition or vain conceit. Rather, in humility value others above yourselves, not looking to your own interests but each of you to the interests of the others."

2. Unity of one heart. This is accomplished through submitting to one another. It has been said that "there can be no union without unity," and that "you may tie the tails of a cat and a dog together by a rope and have union, but you surely don't have unity!"[4] Being connected through force or simply being in the same place is not enough. Hearts must be unified around one purpose and one person —Jesus.

Submission to one another promotes unity of heart. It naturally demolishes any tendency toward ego building. Paul, addressing the brothers and sisters at Colossae, articulates it this way:

Therefore, as God's chosen people, holy and dearly loved, clothe yourselves with compassion, kindness, humility, gentleness and patience. . . . And over all these virtues put on love, which binds them all together in perfect unity.

Let the peace of Christ rule in your hearts, since as members of one body you were called to peace. And be thankful.

—COLOSSIANS 3:12, 14–15

We learn to submit by clothing ourselves in *tender mercies, kindness, humility, meekness (or gentleness), and longsuffering.* As these heart qualities become the worshiper's way of life, their testimony begins to represent the true leadership qualities necessary in developing pathways for unifying the entire team.

In contrast, self-help and motivational experts use different terminology to explain leadership: drive, destiny, ambition, energy, courage, determination, enterprise, hustle, aggressiveness, empire-building, risk-taking, innovation, or entrepreneurialism. But worshipers committed to submission and unity of heart must operate on a totally different plane that prefers and chooses the qualities of lowliness, gentleness, and longsuffering over control, power, or pride.

3. Unity of love. Learning to love each other means learning to bear with each other's weakness while growing in unity. This requires patience and forgiveness. Forbearance "with all love" produces a spirit of unity. Leading a unified group means looking out for the best interest of others.

So how is this done within a worship community? Forbearance will change the atmosphere of the group from worry to trust, suspicion to acceptance, and negativity to optimism. A well-known Christian saying highlights the importance of a life of unity in love and provides a practical guide: "*In essentials, unity. In nonessentials, liberty. In all things, charity.*"

4. Unity in spirit. Scripture encourages us to keep the bond of peace. Peace binds together the body of Christ. It functions like a "superglue" so that relationships are united and woven together.

> And over all these virtues put on love, which binds them all together in perfect unity. Let the peace of Christ rule in your hearts, since as members of one body you were called to peace. And be thankful.
> —COLOSSIANS 3:14–15

This has two layers.

First, the peace of God is to rule the heart. Peace, the aura of mental and emotional serenity, controls the heart. Fear is gone. Anxiety flees. All is well and secure.

Second, this peace becomes a calling bonding us to other believers. It draws individuals into participation in the community.

J. Albert Barnes writes about this internal bonding cultivating a peaceful temperament. He articulates the principles of unity in the bond of peace this way:

> The American Indians usually spoke of peace as a "chain of friendship" which was to be kept bright. The meaning here is, that they should be bound or united together in the sentiments and affections of peace. It is not mere external unity; it is not a mere unity of creed; it is not a mere unity in the forms of public worship; it is such as the Holy Spirit produces in the hearts of Christians, when he fills them all with the same love, and joy, and peace in believing.[5]

This kind of unity of the Spirit is initiated by the Holy Spirit. It is evidenced by a "state of oneness or being in harmony and one accord."[6] It is God's gift for which worshipers should always be grateful.

CHAPTER 19

SERVING

"Great job, guys! Let's pull over in this eddy and see how Steve's raft does." John commended us for safely navigating "Rainbow Falls," a beautifully cascading Class IV rapid. He'd mentioned Steve before, and they seemed to have a longtime friendship cemented by verbal sparring and competition.

"Wow, that was incredible . . . so fun!" Leah commented.

We all chimed in with excitement as we wiped our faces from the spray of the whitewater. It was mid-afternoon, and by now we seemed to be getting the hang of it and longed for more adventure.

Our raft slid over into a slow, swirling eddy by the bank. John spun us sideways so we could look back at Steve's crew hurtling toward Rainbow Falls.

"Uh oh. That's not good. They're coming in from the wrong side. Right forward hard! Ouch!" John shouted as if they could hear him.

He put his hands on his head as we all watched Steve's raft career over the falls sideways and smash into a boulder. The raft pivoted around the rock and started downriver again.

"At least they didn't get stuck," John commented.

Steve and his team paddled hard to get across the current and joined us in the eddy. I noticed a guy in the front slumped over. John immediately sprang into action. He pulled their raft in close. He jumped out in knee-deep water and towed both rafts to shore.

"He hit his head pretty hard on that boulder," Steve said, clearly concerned, as they picked up the drowsy young man and lay him on the beach.

"Take it easy," John said to the loopy rafter as he loosened his life vest.

The young man leaned over and vomited violently all over John.

"Whoa, whoa buddy." John helped him lean over and finish heaving without spraying anyone. "Looks like you got yourself a concussion."

John proceeded to get a towel from his dry bag and wipe the young man off. He got him some fresh water to drink and then splashed river water on his soiled shirt and life vest.

"What's your name?" John asked him.

"Tommy . . . really sorry about getting sick on you. I just got really dizzy."

"Don't sweat it, bud. Take some deep breaths. We are going to get medics out here to take you in and get you evaluated. You'll be alright, but by the looks of that helmet, you rocked your noggin good."

John squeezed his shoulder and dove into the river to clean himself off.

In your relationships with one another, have the same mindset as Christ Jesus: Who, being in very nature God, did not consider equality with God something to be used to his own advantage; rather, he made himself nothing by taking the very nature of a servant, being made in human likeness. And being found in appearance as a man, he humbled himself by becoming obedient to death—even death on a cross!

—PHILIPPIANS 2:5–8

The way of worship is to serve. To serve others is to emulate Jesus. To serve others is to worship Jesus. In serving others, we fulfill our purpose, and when we fulfill our purpose, we are filled with joy unspeakable.

I've heard it said that everyone wants to be thought of as a servant until they are treated like one. So often our wayward hearts spiral into entitlement and self-centeredness. We want to lay claim to things we believe we deserve. It may be a position, title, influence, or privilege. We start to feel like certain things are beneath us. *Let someone else clean the toilet or carry out the trash. That is intern-level stuff. That isn't in my job description.* If we allow these attitudes to take root, pretty soon we aren't serving others or Jesus but instead making decisions solely based on our advancement.

There is nothing wrong with holy ambition or drive to steward what God has given us to do, but left unchecked, that ambition will take us to a place of self-worship and will ultimately distort our lives. Why? Because success cannot satisfy us. Only Jesus can.

Mother Teresa purportedly said, "I see Jesus in every human being. I say to myself, this is hungry Jesus, I must feed him. This is sick Jesus. This one has leprosy or gangrene; I must wash him and tend to him. I serve because I love Jesus."

Our guide, John, did not relegate serving to less experienced interns, apprentices, or the like. He helped us carry our gear. He made us lunch so we could enjoy the canyon. He gathered the trash and disposed of it. He taught us about the river. He affirmed us. He cared for the injured. He helped us. He even let a young man vomit on him while giving him care and didn't even blink! He was more concerned about the welfare of the injured rafter than about himself. He was a decorated adventurer, but he just loved being with us and helping us experience the river. I found out later he had endorsement deals, professional opportunities, and celebrity friends, but he made no mention of it. It was all about serving us on that day. It was all about the river for him.

The Bible tells us that Jesus himself gave us this example, saying, "For even the Son of Man did not come to be served, but to serve, and to give his life as a ransom for many" (Mark 10:45).

If we have artistic gifts in performing and music, many times we are thrust to the forefront, in front of audiences, to display our talent. It can get to our heads and skew our perspective. The audience is facing us. The microphones amplify us. The cameras see us. The lights are focused on us. We stand on an elevated stage. Without even realizing it, we start to think it really is about us. We start to believe the lie that we are the center.

The way of worship calls us to lay our gifts and our very lives on the altar of service. There's no person or task below us. Jesus, the Son of the living God, came to earth as a servant. So in our worship, we do everything unto him, the One who saved us. He is our reward. While we guide others in worship, let's make sure we have the towel of service draped over our arm, ready to run to the need.

Isn't it amazing how so much of what we *do* in worship actually begins with a heart attitude? Serving is the same way. Our service really must begin with a focused heart attitude: *we must be humble in spirit.* Serving others means choosing humility through gracious, generous, considerate actions from the heart. Serving from the heart requires a level of surrender and submission, but the outcome for those who choose it is joy and contentment.

"Serve, served or serving" occurs 214 times in 201 verses in the

New King James Version of the Bible. In the Greek, the word translated "servant" is *diakonos*. The word sometimes refers to a table waiter offering food and drink to guests, preparing food for guests, or to a person supplying an individual or group with the necessities of life. Most often, "servant" denotes a person who occupies some type of subservient role, such as caring for the needs of others rather than for themselves or ministering to the poor.[1]

Consider the Culture

In Mark 10:42–45, two of Jesus's disciples, James and John, ask for the honor and authority of sitting at the right and left hands of the Savior in heaven. Jesus's reply directs the disciples away from the question and to the culture in which they are accustomed to and living: "You know that those who are regarded as rulers of the Gentiles lord it over them, and their high officials exercise authority over them" (Mark 10:42). His intent draws attention to the truth that Jesus's concept of servant leadership is counter to the culture and based upon a completely different nonearthly paradigm.

Honoring others above our own self is just as contrary to the twenty-first century, postmodern, humanistic, secularized culture as it was for those in Greco-Roman culture. Our cultural influences often encourage us to be self-centered and ambitious. In many cases, our drive to achieve prompts us to sacrifice everything (including our relationships with people) for a moment of perceived success. So why should we be surprised that worshipers need to guard against a persona of self-ambition, self-reliance, and self-determination?

Check Your Motive

The gentiles in the disciples' culture were guilty of flaunting their authority, lording over people, and seeking opportunity to be condescending to those perceived as a lower class of people. Jesus strongly rebukes this attitude by saying, "Whoever wants to become great among you must be your servant, and whoever wants to be first must be slave of all" (Mark 10:43–44). He declares that a person desiring leadership will become a servant and a slave themselves. Jesus instructs leaders to be servants, treating others with respect, looking for ways to lift the less fortunate up and care for human needs, and reaching out to the poor and marginalized.

Serving Is Relational

Our worship and service should be driven by our relationship to God (vertical) and with the people around us (horizontal). The dynamic between these two types of relationships enables us to understand the *purpose* for service and worship, the *partnership* between worship and serving, and our *motive* for serving and worship.

Learn from the Best Example

Only after the disciples ask about their position in heaven and Jesus presents them with a new paradigm for leadership does he reveal his deeper motive: "For even the Son of Man did not come to be served, but to serve, and to give His life a ransom for many" (Mark 10:45).

Jesus is the consummate example of servant leadership. He demonstrates how God's concept for serving embraces strong, unselfish relationship. Serving is all about relationship. The worshiper's relationship with God enables one to discover, build, shape, develop, and cultivate relationship with those in every sphere of influence—through service. The apostle Paul provides perspective:

> For by the grace given me I say to every one of you: Do not think of yourself more highly than you ought, but rather think *of yourself* with sober judgment, in accordance with the faith God has distributed to each of you. . . . Do not be proud, but be willing to associate with people of low position. Do not be conceited.
> —ROMANS 12:3, 16; EMPHASIS ADDED

184

Serve Believers

First on the agenda? Paul says, "Be devoted to one another in love. Honor one another above yourselves" (Rom 12:10). For the worshiper, living a lifestyle of service and worship begins with how well they demonstrate love and respect to their brothers and sisters in Christ. It is evidenced by treating everyone fairly, not showing favorites, or honoring the rich and popular above the poor and marginalized.

This is practiced through devotion to one another. This is at the core for serving, building relationships, and establishing unity between believers (Rom 15:9). It is devotion, loyalty, fidelity, dedication, and commitment to each other that makes for successful team building. Joy is found in giving others opportunity to serve. True servant leaders find fulfilment in seeing others become all that God intends for them to be, reaching their goals, growing in grace, and developing their own skills for ministry.

Action Principles for Serving from Romans 12

God is in the process of transforming worshipers, changing them *from old into new*. Worshipers are transformed by the renewing of their mind (Rom 12:2). Why do they go through this process? So that they can better *serve others*. In writing to the believers in Rome, the apostle Paul outlines servant leadership as a ten-fold process:

1. **Serve with humility.** Do not think of yourself more highly than you ought (Romans 12:3).
2. **Serve with grace.** We have different gifts, according to the grace given to each of us (Rom 12:4–6).
3. **Serve with a worshiping spirit.** If your gift is serving, then serve (Rom 12:7).
4. **Serve generously.** If your gift is giving, then give generously (Rom 12:8).

5. **Serve with gladness.** If your gift is to show mercy, do it cheerfully (Rom 12:8b).

6. **Serve in love.** Your love must be sincere. Be devoted to one another in love. Honor one another above yourselves (Rom 12:9–10).

7. **Serve the Lord and other people.** Never lack zeal, but keep your spiritual fervor, serving the Lord. Share with the Lord's people who are in need and practice hospitality (Rom 12:11, 13).

8. **Serve unselfishly.** Bless those who persecute you, rejoice with those who rejoice, mourn with those who mourn (Rom 12:12–15).

9. **Serve without discrimination.** Live in harmony with one another. Do not be proud, but be willing to associate with people of low position. Do not be conceited (Rom 12:16).

10. **Serve without expectation or reprisal.** Do not repay anyone evil for evil. Be careful to do what is right in the eyes of everyone. Do not take revenge, my dear friends, but leave room for God's wrath (Rom 12:17, 19).

Romans 12:8 tells us, "If [your gift] is to lead, do it diligently." So how do our lives demonstrate to those around us that we are servant worshipers? We demonstrate our love for and service to others, become the hands and feet of Jesus, and are driven by passion for God and love for others.

Our service must be genuine and sincere (Rom 12:9). Our actions are the fruit of our worship of and time spent with God. We are to reach out to believer and unbeliever alike, love them, serve them, and seek to build lasting relationships. Guidelines for serving become principles for leadership.

Obedience to that mission is driven by a deep love for Jesus. In the words of the apostle Paul, "If your enemy is hungry, feed him; if he is thirsty, give him something to drink. . . . Do not be overcome by evil, but overcome evil with good" (Rom 12:20–21). For the person seeking to follow the way of worship, serving begins with a humble attitude, prompted by the Holy Spirit and transformed into action as God provides opportunities to minister. The worshiper's attitude of servant worship prompts obedience through service.

In the final analysis, as a worshiper, serving is both a calling and a gift. God calls worshipers to serve, and he then equips them with unique gifts according to the grace given to each individual (Rom 12:6). Genuine, heart-motivated, Christ-glorifying service opens the door for the worshiper to reach, impact, and influence the culture. The servant leader diligently casts aside selfish ambition and gives preference to obeying the call for collaboration in service and to developing a team of servant leaders dedicated to fulfilling the call to lead God's people in worship.

CHAPTER 20

SACRIFICING

Before we left that day, we waited in the cool, crisp morning air for our guides to show up. My eyes perused the walls of the camp office. Newspaper articles, Polaroid photos, vintage life vests, and wooden oars adorned the cedar-paneled walls. It had the feel of a small-town museum of sorts. One of the framed newspaper headlines caught my eye.

"Local Family Buys Whitewater Camp,
Vows to Protect History."

Below the headline was a weathered black-and-white photo of a curly headed man, probably in his twenties, holding a paddle out toward the camera. He was squinting from the sun and grinning from ear to ear. His tank top revealed his muscular arms. I only got about two sentences into the article when I was interrupted.

"Hey, it's Michael, right?" John asked as he walked in.

"Yep, that's me." I turned around.

"I have to grab some things out of the shed. Could you give me a hand?" John asked.

"Sure thing." I looked at Leah and mouthed to her that I'd be right back.

We walked out the side screen door and onto the gravel path that wound toward the river. My hiking shoes crunched the tiny rocks with every step. Birds chirped in the trees, and the river bubbled along at the base of the hill. The path narrowed, lined with beautiful fir and pine trees of several varieties. It was magical.

"So what line of work are you in?" John asked.

"Music. I'm from Florida, but I live in Nashville now. Trying to make a go of it like every other person in that town."

"Cool! I play a mean ukulele, but that's about it. I think I know three songs." John chuckled.

"Right on! If you can play three, I bet you can play a lot more." I craned my neck to look at the beauty in every direction. "Man, this place sure is stunning. I noticed that article in the office about the family buying the camp. Was that your dad in the picture?"

"Yeah, that's him. It's an incredible story really. He took extra work in construction, worked like three jobs, and sold everything he could to buy this place thirty years ago. He always told me anything worth having will take sacrifice. There's a great quote he made me memorize from an old Baptist missionary, Adoniram Judson, that says, 'There is no success without sacrifice. If you succeed without sacrifice it is because someone has suffered before you. If you sacrifice without success it is because someone will succeed after.'"

"Man, that's powerful," I said. I was caught off guard by the immediate, profound conversation.

"He is so passionate about the river," John said. "He really wanted to care for this land. He wanted something to pass down to the generations ahead of him. Nearly everything you see around here he built with his own hands. His mission is to help as many people as possible fall in love with the river."

"Is that your mission too?" I asked.

"Yeah, you could say that. When you find something so amazing, you want others to experience it too. Whatever you have to give up to live out that purpose, it's no sacrifice at all really. It's just joy . . . all joy."

"So you've given some stuff up then?"

"Just stuff." John replied with a grin. "It's a lot . . . you know, to take care of this place, to manage the business, and to prepare yourself for the river physically and mentally. It definitely costs you. It's a price worth paying, though. You'll see."

Then he said to them all: "Whoever wants to be my disciple must deny themselves and take up their cross daily and follow me. For whoever wants to save their life will lose it, but whoever loses their life for me will save it."

—LUKE 9:23–24

To sacrifice is to give up something for the sake of something better. To sacrifice is to put something to death so something else can live. The way of worship is, by God's grace and the power of the Holy Spirit, dethroning us from our hearts and enthroning God. That means something has to die. That something is me. Something has to be given up for the sake of something worthier. The way of worship says, "Whatever the cost, I will follow." To love God and worship him fully, there will be sacrifice. Tim Keller says, "The gospel is this: We are more sinful and flawed in ourselves than we ever dared believe, yet at the very same time we are more loved and accepted in Jesus than we ever dared hope."[1] In light of the gospel, in light of this grace, mercy, and love, there is no sacrifice too great.

When we worship, when we sit at his feet and enumerate the countless facets of the diamond that he is, we are caught up in who and what we were created for: relationship with him. The way of worship will cost us our time, our treasure, our deepest effort, and our willful perseverance. It will cost us endless hours of study, practice, and preparation. It will require listening and counseling, detailed planning, and sometimes excruciating confrontation. It will cost us the approval of men and a strained song in the deepest grief. To care for the least, to serve the desperate and destitute, and to love those who cannot reciprocate—this is the sacrificial way of worship. It will cost us everything.

But in losing everything, we overflow with more than enough. This is the confounding mystery of the love of God. He is our reward. We belong to him, and he belongs to us!

Let's not be fooled into thinking our worship of the Lord won't cost us. It costs us everything, and yet we lack nothing. John's father was willing to do whatever it took, to plant deep roots for his family at the river. He wanted to help as many as possible experience the life-giving joy of the waters. May we do the same in our sacred calling as worshipers of the Most High, whatever it costs.

> But the king replied to Araunah, "No, I insist on paying you for it. I will not sacrifice the LORD my God burnt offerings that cost me nothing." So David bought the threshing floor and the oxen and paid fifty shekels of silver for them. David built an altar to the LORD there and sacrificed burnt offerings and fellowship offerings. Then the LORD answered his prayer in behalf of the land, and the plague on Israel was stopped.
>
> —2 SAMUEL 24:24–25

The command to sacrifice appears, on the surface, to be somewhat simple: offer to God our sacrifice. It seems a bit strange that God—who has everything, knows everything, doesn't need anyone, created all things, and is enthroned in the heavenlies—wants our sacrifice. And what kind of sacrifice does he desire?

In a July 2004 blog, Billy Graham suggested that the sacrifice in the Old Testament, according to Galatians 3:24, had a variety of goals: (1) to impart important truths; (2) to serve God more efficiently; (3) to prepare for the coming of Jesus Christ, the Messiah; (4) to explain the seriousness of sin; (5) to communicate that God is holy; (6) to clarify that sin must be judged; and (7) to demonstrate God's mercy and grace.[2] Graham continued by explaining that because of Jesus's sacrifice on the cross, the Old Testament practice of killing animals for the atonement of sin are no longer needed: "But he has appeared once for all . . . to do away with sin by the sacrifice of himself" (Heb 9:26).[3]

God wants us to become *living sacrifices* of praise to him. Learning to lay ourselves down on the altar requires the foundation laid in the previous chapters—calling, spirit and truth, thankfulness, character, brokenness, humility, integrity, equipping, and empowering.

Why, if Jesus has once for all done away with the "sacrifice," does Hebrews urge, if not require, New Testament believers to "offer to God our sacrifice"? In fact, the admonition is to "continually offer sacrifice from lips that speak his name." For the worshiper, these "continual" sacrifices take place at all times, in all places, and in all circumstances—when experiencing joy or dealing with sadness in all seasons of life. In one true sense, the "continual sacrifices" provide a template for the worshiper to demonstrate lifestyle worship.

Criteria of a Sacrifice

Under the Old Testament system, there are many types of sacrifices for various purposes. In the New Testament, Christ is the "one" sacrifice for all times and for all people—no more sacrifices are necessary for the atonement of sin. In the Old Testament, sacrifices are made with an expectation of receiving something in return: forgiveness for sins committed, provisions, cleansing, atonement, a memorial for a miracle, or victory over the enemy.

New Testament believers no longer sacrifice in order to get something. They are already co-heirs with Christ and recipients of his gifts, mercies, fellowship, grace, and more. Sacrifices are given in response for all that God has already done through the person of Jesus Christ. Christ becomes the center and turning point of the worshiper's entire life.

In the Old Testament, symbolism, structure, sacrifice, and service regulate tabernacle or temple worship practices. God chooses to dwell in the holy of holies, and men and women may only approach God through a priest, a human mediator. In the New Testament, grace and mercy regulate worship practices. God chooses to dwell in the human heart, and a new covenant establishes each believer as a kingdom priest—with Jesus himself as high priest.

It is a requirement that Old Testament sacrifices be undefiled, perfect, without blemish, and representative of the very best one could offer unto the Lord. In the New Testament, everything is about transformation of the heart—motive, ambition, life focus, and desires. And the sacrifice for the believer to offer to God themselves as a "living sacrifice" includes all our desires.

Today, God sees his people through the lens of grace and the shed blood of his Son, Jesus. As worshipers are sanctified and transformed in their mind through the Holy Spirit living in them, worship becomes a representation of their time alone with Jesus, love for righteousness and holy living, faith in God, and commitment to a lifestyle of worship.

Cost of the Sacrifice

King David made a commitment to present to God only that which represents true, honest, and worthy sacrifice. David says, "No, I insist on paying you for it. I will not sacrifice to the LORD my God burnt offerings that cost me nothing."

While our sacrifices as Christ followers no longer require the killing of lambs, fowl, bulls, and oxen, God does require worshipers to give of their very best to him. Our sacrifices need to cost us something, or they are not really sacrifices at all. The sacrifices must be from hearts full of love for the Lord, and nothing should be expected in return.

What, you might ask, am I going to sacrifice? There are many things you can and should sacrifice to God as a worship leader. Perhaps the following four areas provide a starting place for unselfish sacrifice to the Lord.

1. **Time.** Be available to practice, prepare, perform, and provide worship as unto the Lord and whenever opportunities become available. No opportunity is too small.
2. **Talents.** We do not own our talents. God graciously loans us our talents for us to steward, and we should give them back to the Lord with a willing heart and unselfish spirit. God quietly removes the gifts from our spirit and lives when we fail to steward, develop, and nurture those gifts for the glory of God and the testimony of Jesus Christ.
3. **Treasure.** We should view our money not as our possession but as a loan we are to invest wisely in the kingdom. Our Lord promises to supply all needs according to his riches in Christ Jesus.
4. **Life.** The Bible teaches that worshipers should offer their bodies as a living sacrifice, holy and pleasing to God. This is true and proper worship (Rom 12:1).

Results

We may not need to sacrifice animals at an altar anymore, but God still expects us to offer him sacrifices that represent our daily walk with him. How is this made practical in the worshiper's life? The writer of Hebrews articulates the parameters for living a life of continual praise. He suggests that we should openly profess his name, and in the process he offers five practical scenarios for continually offering God sacrifice:

> Through Jesus, therefore, let us *continually* offer to God a *sacrifice of praise*—the fruit of lips that openly profess his name. And do not forget to do good and to share with others, for with such sacrifices God is pleased. . . . Pray for us. . . . Now may the God of peace . . . equip you [make you complete] with everything good for doing his will, and may he work in us what is pleasing to him, through Jesus Christ, to whom be glory for ever and ever. Amen.
> —HEBREWS 13:15–16, 18, 20–21; EMPHASIS ADDED

Sacrifice of Praise

Notice that the sacrifice of praise continually presents the fruit of worshiping lips. Did you know that this kind of sacrifice most clearly represents the heart? Jesus's understanding of the relationship between that which is coming from the mouth and heart is stated in Luke's gospel:

> A good man brings good things out of the good stored up in his heart, and an evil man brings evil things out of the evil stored up in his heart. For the mouth speaks what the heart is full of.
> —LUKE 6:45

The songwriter Asaph reminds us that our sacrifices of praise must come from the heart and that worshipers should guard and protect that which comes into our lives through the ears, eyes, mind, and heart: "Above all else, guard your heart, for everything you do flows from it" (Prov 4:23).

Sacrifice of Thanksgiving

Give thanks! Again, thanksgiving is from the fruit of our lips. In fact, the Bible says that the fruit of our lips begins with giving thanks. The psalmist writes, "He who offers a sacrifice of thanksgiving honors Me and to him who orders his way aright I shall show the salvation of God" (Ps 50:23 NASB).

Interestingly, there is a rabbinical tradition that teaches that all the Mosaic sacrifices would have a beginning and an end except the thank offering, and all prayers would cease except the prayer of thanksgiving! This is why the biblical instruction to continually offer up sacrifices to the Lord is so important. Our prayers of thanksgiving should never cease!

Sacrifice of Righteousness

This has everything to do with character, right living, being honorable, and fleeing the temptation to sin. It begins in the heart. Trust God to protect your heart. Commit your heart in all that you do (including worship) to the Lord, and he will direct your path, exalt you in his own time, and settle your heart. The psalmist puts the principle into a song: "Offer the sacrifices of the righteous and trust in the LORD" (Ps 4:5).

Sacrifice of Prayer

We should be willing to spend our time and devote our hearts to the needs of another. God's Word calls intercession a sacrifice: "Pray for us. We are sure that we have a clear conscience and desire to live honorably in every way" (Heb 13:18).

Sacrifice of Peace

The writer of Colossians writes, "Let the peace of Christ *rule in your hearts,* since as members of one body you were *called to peace.* And *be thankful*" (Col 3:15).

The results of a worshiper deliberately living the life of sacrifice is profound. God's Word promises that if you practice a lifestyle of sacrificial worship, the God of peace will show himself strong in your life. Note that the instruction is to let the peace of Christ rule in our hearts. We are called to peace, and the result is thanksgiving. The psalmist puts this in perspective: "In peace I will lie down and sleep, for you alone, Lord, make me dwell in safety" (Ps 4:8).

Remember, it is the Holy Spirit that makes the worshiper complete, so that the will of God may be accomplished. And your life, as a worshiper, will be transformed by the renewing of your mind. Then you will be able to test and approve what God's will is: his good, pleasing, and perfect will. Trust God to do his good work as you faithfully offer to him your sacrifices of peace.

CHAPTER 21

CRAFT

"You guys got quiet on me. Everybody okay?" John asked as we rode in the van up the curling switchbacks to our launch destination that morning.

"Could somebody crack a window? I'm a little nauseous," Neal proclaimed from the back bench seat.

"Seriously, someone open a window," Franny chimed in as she rolled her eyes.

The windows flew open in record time.

I changed the subject. "John, so how long did it take you to become a guide?"

"Well, it didn't take too long to learn the basics and become certified at the lowest levels. I had a head start with being around it so much with my father." He paused. "There's a big difference in initially getting certified and being a master guide, though. I guess we're kind of like doctors. There are doctors who just get a medical degree, and then there are doctors you'll trust your life with."

"So I'm praying you're the latter."

"Ha ha! Of course, but we shall see."

"Have you run any whitewater outside North America?" I asked.

"Oh yeah. Exploring is important. It keeps you fresh. There's some gnarly stuff out there. You don't grow unless you explore."

"What are some of your favorites?"

"Let's see, there are so many . . . I love Karnali in Nepal, Rio Upano in Ecuador, the White Nile in Uganda, too, though I'm not a fan of the crocs."

"Seriously, crocs? Nope, nope, nope," I said emphatically. "Any close calls?"

"I've done some stupid stuff, but not anymore. I'll explore, but only where my craft can handle it."

"You mean your ability?"

"Yeah. I take my craft very seriously. My fitness, technique, knowledge—anything I *can* prepare for, I will prepare for."

I was growing more confident about the adventure that lay ahead. If this guy was in the boat with us, we'd be good. "How long do you feel like it took you before you felt ready?" I asked. He didn't even have to think about it.

"A thousand evaluated hours."

"Evaluated hours?"

"Yeah. Everyone can get reps once they're certified, and that's really important—just running rivers as much and as often as you can. The great ones, though, get with the masters and instructors and allow themselves to be evaluated so they can really hone their craft."

"So a thousand hours of masters and instructors evaluating and teaching you?"

"You got to stay humble and hungry if you really want to experience the good stuff safely. I see some of these other yahoos taking people down the river who have no business guiding. They don't take it seriously. It never ends well. Those who chase it . . . those are the ones who really honor the river and those they guide. It's the only way."

"Chase what?" I asked.

He smiled wildly with his hand draped over the steering wheel. "The very best version of everything."

The workers labored faithfully. Over them to direct them were Jahath and Obadiah, Levites descended from Merari, and Zechariah and Meshullam, descended from Kohath. The Levites—all who were skilled in playing musical instruments—had charge of the laborers and supervised all the workers from job to job. Some of the Levites were secretaries, scribes and gatekeepers.

—2 CHRONICLES 34:12–13

Everything we do is for Jesus. We lead, we serve, we learn, we work, we sing, we prepare, we rest, we plan, we give, and we love—all for him. The journey to master the skills of the work of our hands is an integral part of the way of worship. It is part of our offering, our response to the One who is worthy of it all. The stakes couldn't be higher. For those spiritual practitioners leading in the church, if we are not prepared—if we do not know our craft—we will distract and dishonor our Creator, and we will not only lead poorly, but we will lead those with us astray. A casual and lazy approach to gifts that God has blessed us with is no way to honor the Lord. This is a stewardship issue.

Albert Einstein supposedly said, "Only one who devotes himself to a cause with his whole strength and soul can be a true master. For this reason, mastery demands all of a person." What does it take to chase the "very best version of everything"? It requires a sense of humility that says, "I do not know everything I need to know" and an abiding willingness to invite and assimilate instruction. We need to seek out those who can see ways we need to change, improve, and grow, and help us put those things into practice.

We hear a lot about excellence. One of my mentors, coach Tom Mullins, says, "Excellence is doing your very best all of the time. Excellence honors God and removes distraction." I love that. When we strive to master our craft as musicians, technicians, fine artists, preachers, teachers, leaders, and the like, we honor God in our pursuit. It's not perfection; it's pursuit. We will never master our craft without practice. But we can't just practice for practice's sake. We have to practice the *right* things.

Practice alone *does not* make perfect. It does make permanent. In my early years of studying piano, I always wanted to spend the most time on the section of the Bach fugue that I knew. It sounded so good. I felt powerful and accomplished. It was fun and satisfying. It's helpful to feel that sense of confidence and accomplishment fuel us when we get discouraged, but we cannot get stuck playing the only section we know over and over. We fool ourselves into thinking we know the whole piece. When the recital comes, disaster ensues.

Psalm 33:3 instructs us to "sing to him a new song; play skillfully, and shout for joy." John realized running the river was a privilege, honor, and joy. It was not a hobby or something to be taken lightly. It was dangerous, exciting, and full of adventure. It truly was a life and death situation every day. Whatever the discipline and gifting we have, we must chase the very best version of our craft. The Lord deserves nothing less, and in serving him, neither do the people we care for, serve, and guide.

> Love so amazing so divine
> Demands my soul, my life, my all.
> —ISAAC WATTS, "WHEN I SURVEY
> THE WONDROUS CROSS"

We have explored how personal character and integrity are important to the way of worship and how to develop community and fellowship as leaders. We have discussed how worship is a calling that must be pursued with a specific heart attitude. But now we are going to examine two additional principles critical for leading worship—craft and competence.

The Worshiper's Obligation

What does it mean to develop craft and competence?

> And whatever you do in word or deed, do all in the name of the Lord Jesus, giving thanks to God the Father through him . . . with sincerity of heart and reverence for the Lord. Whatever you do, work at it with all your heart, as working for the Lord.
> —COLOSSIANS 3:17, 22–23

Craft or skill refers to a natural, God-given talent, and it may be one of the reasons you became interested in leading worship in the first place. It is the innate, inborn, or instinctive talent or skill set to accomplish something. A craft is any activity that requires intentionally honing a specific set of skills, from pottery, carpentry, and woodworking to music, writing, and painting. Craft or skill can also refer to having a set of skills even if you are not specifically creating something, like a skilled warrior, physician, or river guide. Craft can also apply to having the natural skill or talent to perform—as in the case of the arts.[1]

The Bible has a great deal to say about God using those that have a natural craft or skill. In fact, the Hebrew word for "skill" (*sâkal*) is used sixty-five times in sixty-three verses in the King James Version. *Skill* is sometimes used synonymously with "prosper, have understanding, wisdom, and instruct." There are actually three ways this word, *skill* or *craft*, may be used.

1. As a noun, it is used in the sense of knowledge (Eccl 9:11), insight (Dan 1:17), or wisdom (1 Chron 28:21). So in this way, it means understanding.

2. As an adjective, it refers to the manner of doing a thing, devising, or planning.

3. It can also refer to the training that makes one skilled. Skillfulness (Ps 78:72) is used with reference to the hands not only in their work but also in guidance. For example, the scriptural rendering for "skillfully" in Psalm 33:3 translates "to play well." "Unskillful," as used in Hebrews 5:13, is used to describe a sense of inexperience.[2]

Two Old Testament examples underline how important skilled craftsmen were in temple worship. First, in 1 Chronicles 15:22, Kenaniah, the head Levite, was placed in charge of all the singing because he was skilled.

Second, King David, together with the commanders of the army, set apart some of the sons of Asaph, Heman and Jeduthun, for the ministry of prophesying, accompanied by harps, lyres, and cymbals:

> All these men were under the supervision of their father for the music of the temple of the LORD, with cymbals, lyres and harps, for the ministry at the house of God. Asaph, Jeduthun and Heman were under the supervision of the king. Along with their relatives—all of them trained and skilled in music for the LORD—they numbered 288. Young and old alike, teacher as well as student.
>
> —1 CHRONICLES 25:6–7

When applied to worship, the talent God bestows on each worship leader is "given as Christ apportioned it" (Eph 4:7). The Bible teaches that "every good and perfect gift is from above, coming down from the Father of the heavenly lights" (James 1:17). No matter the talent, God expects you to develop, nurture, cultivate, and grow that skill as a testimony of his grace. This developing and growing process is where competence comes in.

Competence refers to the product or outcome of developing, nurturing, or growing talent. A competent person is qualified to perform a task well. Competence is gained through education, training, experience, and opportunity combined with a person's natural ability.

Worship leaders must be committed to developing competence and to present themselves as ones "approved," as skilled, competent, able, and quality workers so that they may perform their skill or craft with excellence—every time they are called upon to do so (2 Tim 2:15). For worship leaders, it means there must be consistent, conscientious, and intentional time spent developing themselves as serious and skilled artists—musicians, songwriters, singers, guitarists, conductors, drummers, pianists, percussionists, sound engineers, lighting technicians, painters, set designers, graphic designers, and more.

Craft is your natural talent and ability. Competence is that talent developed or matured. Competence is usually a reflection of the amount of effort, time, energy, focus, and dedication a person has given to developing their talent or gift.

How do we develop our talents? Sometimes God places in the life of the worshiper a mentor specifically given the responsibility to teach, train, and shape the worship leader's talent. At other times, God gives opportunity for the worshiper to develop craft or skill as an apprentice or intern. There are times the Lord opens doors for worshipers to receive formal training. Remember, when God calls, he obligates himself to help equip the called person to serve.

The Worshiper's Opportunity

Although the spiritual formation mentioned in the previous chapters is essential to successful worship ministry, you and I, as called-out worship leaders, must also be skilled (talented) and competent (trained) to do that which God has called us to do with excellence.

A worship leader must have developed his or her natural talent and skill (craft) to the level of competence necessary for directing or managing worship presentations with excellence. The Bible demonstrates the connection between motives and skill with the life of King David: "David shepherded them with integrity of heart; with skillful hands he led them" (Ps 78:72).

Robert Morgan tells a story about Billy Graham and Cliff Barrows, music evangelist for the Graham Team for many decades:

> It seems that Billy Graham was to speak for a Youth for Christ Rally at Ben Lippen Conference Center in Asheville, North Carolina, in the summer of 1944. It was a Saturday evening, and the youth service was to begin at 7:30 p.m. The congregation was gathered and patiently waiting for the service to begin. The host of the event was waiting patiently for the worship leader (song director and master of ceremonies) to arrive. Soon it was 7:35 p.m. and no worship leader. Then, it was 7:45 p.m. and still no one to lead worship. The congregants were getting restless, beginning to look at their watches. It then was 8:00 p.m. and no worship leader. Finally, the host of the evening walked to the podium and asked if there was anyone in the congregation who could help lead in some choruses and songs before the guest preacher of the evening would speak. Twenty-two-year-old Cliff Barrows and his wife, Billie, were on their honeymoon and just happened to be at the conference meeting. A friend, Albert Brown, encouraged Cliff to raise his hand and volunteer. Cliff asked the host to give him a minute to quickly retrieve his trombone from his car. Cliff led worship while his new bride played the piano. It was at that moment that the Lord placed Cliff Barrows in front of Billy Graham and the two became ministry partners for the next fifty years. Cliff Barrows' prior preparation provided opportunity that literally changed the direction of his life's career and shaped the entire presentation of music and worship for the Billy Graham Crusade events for decades to come.[3]

The worship leader must be equally skilled and competent as an artist (music, dance, art, etc.) and in spiritual truth (teacher, proclaimer, mentor, edifier). When this level of competence is achieved, God begins to open doors of opportunity for the equipping of the saints for the work of ministry and the edifying of the body of Christ (Eph 4:12). The writer of Proverbs 22:29 places this issue of craft and competence in proper prospective:

> Do you see someone *skilled* in their work?
>> They will serve before kings;
>> they will not serve before officials of low rank.
>> —PROVERBS 22:29; EMPHASIS ADDED

D. HIS WORK, OUR RELATIONSHIPS

CHAPTER 22

COMMUNICATION

"Okay guys, circle up here before we head back out," John said as he motioned us over. "I've got some info for you on this next rapid. Remember what I told you about the guy that drowned? That rapid is coming up. You're going to want to pay attention."

We were all completely dialed in. "We must go in fast and straight on. If you follow my commands, we won't have any issue. I haven't had any swimmers here, so don't worry. I just need to make sure you hear me and follow me. It's a really fun and exciting rapid!"

"How did it happen again?" I asked.

"He fought the river. After he fell in, he panicked and kept trying to crawl up onto a rock, which actually put him in the dead center of the haystack. Before they could get to him, he exhausted himself, and that was it." He addressed us all. "*If* you fall in, don't panic, and don't fight the river. She will cough you up and send you downstream. If you are stuck under the water, make the paddle an extension of your arms. Hold the blade, and put the T-grip of the paddle as high above you as possible. We'll come get you." He demonstrated with his own paddle. "Everybody good?"

We all nodded in solemn agreement. "Well, it's been nice getting to know ya," Neal mumbled to me.

We loaded up and paddled back out into the gentle flow. It only took us a couple of minutes before the canyon narrowed, and the water really began to churn. My pulse quickened. None of us said a word as we hung on every command from John. Up and down our raft jolted over the waves. "Forward hard!" John yelled.

We cascaded down a huge wave and then up the other side. The nose of our raft catapulted into the air. A wall of water then crashed over Neal and me in the front. We all dug in and pulled through. It was exhilarating.

"Swimmer! Swimmer!" John yelled. I didn't quite comprehend what was happening.

I turned around to celebrate with Leah, and she had vanished. One minute she was behind me paddling and cheering. The next, she was gone. I looked at John, and I saw an intensity and concern on his face I hadn't seen before.

What's happening? Is she okay?

John quickly had us spin the boat over into an eddy. We looked across the torrent of whitewater. There was no sign of her. The seconds ticked by, and I watched helplessly in disbelief.

"There she is!" Anastasia shouted and pointed. In the center of the river you could see about six inches of the T-grip of her paddle rising just out of the water. We positioned the raft and headed back upstream. John pulled out his rescue throw-bag and stood up in the raft. After about fifteen seconds her tiny body catapulted up on a rapid like a fishing bobber. She looked so small, like a rag doll being tossed on the top of the waves. We immediately headed back out into the flow and were able to grab her and pull her into the boat about thirty yards downstream. She was fine, unfazed even. I realized how quickly things can change.

That rapid marked me for life.

The tongue of the wise adorns knowledge,
but the mouth of the fool gushes folly.
—PROVERBS 15:2

Clear, courageous communication is foundational in leading and guiding people in the way of worship. Why? Because communication is essential in relationships. Effective communication creates unity. When we communicate clearly, lovingly, and truthfully, we grow trust in the garden of our relationships: trust that our words mean something, trust that we have the very best in mind for those we love and lead. In guiding, we must communicate where we are going and why.

John was an extraordinary communicator. He let us know what was coming. He taught us how to handle it. He warned us of danger and constantly pointed to the beauty of what we were experiencing. He took our raft full of very different people, from all walks of life and with very different personalities and abilities, and made us a unified group of adventurers. His clear instruction brought stability to our journey.

As leaders, so often we make assumptions that those on the journey with us know what we are thinking, are already prepared, or think like we do. That sets us up for poor communication. John cared about our safety and our unity, and he cared about us. He knew if we were not together, we wouldn't make it. His clear, direct communication about the river, our paddling techniques, and what lay ahead not only kept us unified, it kept us safe. Leah's life was spared due to his wise and diligent communication. He made sure we understood the gravity of what was happening. He took it seriously yet helped us have fun. He told us of the danger but gave us the tools to navigate safely. Even with disaster always lurking, we were together, we were unified, and we were prepared.

Thankfully, he made no assumptions that day, he wasn't worried about what we thought, and he cared enough to speak the truth.

As worship leaders, we must learn to do the same.

> Instead, speaking the truth in love, we will grow to become in every respect the mature body of him who is the head, that is, Christ. From him the whole body, joined and held together by every supporting ligament, grows and builds itself up in love, as each part does its work.
> —EPHESIANS 4:15–16

Communication is both so central to human life and so difficult that it is an entire discipline, an industry, and one of the most popular majors in colleges and universities around the globe. There are formal undergraduate, graduate, and doctoral degrees in science communication, organizational communication, behavioral communication, business communications, mass communications, sports communications, and more. There are "informal" workshops and seminars hosted by well-known personalities that promote methodology for building great communication skills.

The list of places where communication skills are valuable seems endless. So why should we be surprised if it is important for worship leaders as well? Good communication for a worship team is rooted in our earlier conversations about relationship, team, stewardship, submission, obedience, character, and trust.

In this chapter, we are going to focus on a specific area of skilled communication: managing the tongue. There are five areas of communication that spring from a person's heart: holy, humble, honest, harmful, and healthy communication.

Holy Communication

How we use our tongue is clearly important to God. The epistle of James devotes almost an entire chapter in his epistle to the subject of controlling our tongues. James specifically articulates the need for believers to discipline themselves in the way they communicate to one another:

> Those who consider themselves religious and yet do not keep a tight rein on their tongues deceive themselves, and their religion is worthless. . . . but no human being can tame the tongue. It is a restless evil, full of deadly poison. With the tongue we praise our Lord and Father, and with it we curse human beings, who have been made in God's likeness. Out of the same mouth come praise and cursing. My brothers and sisters, this should not be. Can both fresh water and salt water flow from the same spring?
> —JAMES 1:26; 3:8–11

The psalmist pens similar sentiments when describing the evil in the heart of his enemy: "With their mouths they bless, but in their hearts they curse" (Ps 62:4). The worshiper has the responsibility to discipline himself and guard communication processes. How might the worshiper guard and develop holy communication?

We are instructed in Scripture to flee, or run away, from evil, and this is just as true for how we speak. The psalmist provides at least two principles for fleeing from the temptation to misuse our words.

First, it begins with the purpose of the worshiper's heart. The psalmist writes, "You have tested my heart; You have visited *me* in the night; You have tried me and have found nothing; *I have purposed that my mouth* shall not transgress" (Ps 17:3 NKJV; emphasis added).

Second, we flee evil by guarding our tongues. The psalmist writes, "keep your tongue from evil and your lips from telling lies. Turn from evil and do good; seek peace and pursue it" (Ps 34:13).

There are numerous ways to flee evil communication, but the temptation to speak in sinful ways is sometimes overwhelming. Perhaps the most efficient method for guarding your tongue is to practice using your speech well through private and public exaltation of God. Brag on God. Proclaim the wonders of God to the nations. Present sacrifices of praise to God. The Psalms provide at least three examples: extol the Lord, tell of his deeds, and sing praises:

> I cried out to him with my mouth;
>> his praise was on my tongue.
>> —PSALM 66:17

> I will give thanks to you, Lord, with all my heart;
>> I will tell of all your wonderful deeds.
>> —PSALM 9:1

> The Lord is my strength and my shield;
>> my heart trusts in him, and he helps me.
> My heart leaps for joy,
>> and with my song I praise him.
>> —PSALM 28:7

But holy communication doesn't just mean avoiding evil. It also means seeking to edify others by instructing and encouraging them. Encouragement means taking the time to support each other and speak hope, confidence, inspiration, and truth to each other.

> When you come together, each of you has a hymn, or a word of instruction, a revelation, a tongue or an interpretation. Everything must be done so that the church may be built up.
>> —1 CORINTHIANS 14:26

> These things I remember
>> as I pour out my soul:
> how I used to go to the house of God
>> under the protection of the Mighty One

with shouts of joy and praise
among the festive throng.
—PSALM 42:4

Praise the LORD. I will extol the LORD with all my heart in the
council of the upright and in the assembly.
—PSALM 111:1

Be filled with the Spirit, speaking to one another with psalms, hymns,
and songs from the Spirit. Sing and make music from your heart to
the Lord.
—EPHESIANS 5:18–19

Humble Communication

We have discussed humility before. It means to be modest, or the opposite of prideful. It is important to be modest in conversation, presentation, and communication. Refuse to take the opportunity to brag about your skills or accomplishments. Worshipers must never think more highly of themselves than others. Instead, we must quietly serve and be genuine in our instruction and encouragement.

May the Lord silence all flattering lips
and every boastful tongue
—PSALM 12:3

My mouth will speak words of wisdom;
the meditation of my heart will give you understanding.
—PSALM 49:3

To humans belong the plans of the heart,
but from the LORD comes the proper answer of the tongue.
—PROVERBS 16:1

Do not boast about tomorrow,
>for you do not know what a day may bring.
Let someone else praise you, and not your own mouth;
>an outsider, and not your own lips.
>>—PROVERBS 27:1–2

Look at the implications for communication from one of the most significant song writing groups in the Bible, the family of Korah:

My heart is stirred by a noble theme
>as I recite my verses for the king;
>my tongue is the pen of a skillful writer.
>>—PSALM 45:1

Honest Communication

Just as humble communication begins in the heart of the worshiper, so too does honest communication. Honesty relies on the Holy Spirit to transform from the inside out:

I said, "I will watch my ways
>and keep my tongue from sin;
I will put a muzzle on my mouth
>while in the presence of the wicked."
>>—PSALM 39:1

The tongue of the wise adorns knowledge,
>but the mouth of the fool gushes folly. . . .
The soothing tongue is a tree of life,
>but a perverse tongue crushes the spirit.
>>—PROVERBS 15:2, 4

Honest communication means speaking your testimony of God's goodness in your life.

Testimony gives an open example of how the worshiper speaks in love, sings with grace, and serves with humility. Being honest about your testimony establishes your reputation. Testimony is an open reflection of the heart and at the center of successful communication.

Honest communication displays your temperament and keeps you from putting up a false front. Temperament has to do with a person's nature, disposition, character, or personality, especially as it permanently affects their behavior. Testimony has to do with what people see; temperament is how others experience you in relationship.

Christian Eilers puts these issues of temperament into perspective when dealing with hindrances to good communication:

> Don't scream, make passive-aggressive comments, or sigh in frustration. This will only create ill will toward you and will not set things on the right track. Instead, be patient and kind in your feedback, and you'll keep relationships intact and have the issue resolved.[1]

Harmful Communication

It is no secret that communication that is full of pride and arrogance divides and destroys. Sometimes it's evident by the way worshipers respond to each other, when they give and receive correction with a contrary spirit. Feedback is important, but if not wielded carefully, it can cause great harm. Our words are powerful, and if we don't use them well, they can cause destruction.

Criticism, no matter how justified, will hurt and wound if it is not communicated with love and grace. Worship leaders must not be critical, harsh, or vindictive. Oswald Chambers explains more clearly the danger in using communication as a means for criticism and divisiveness. Using Matthew 7:1–5 and Romans 2:17–24 as a biblical starting place, Chambers provides exhortation on how worshipers can overcome harmful communication:

> Jesus' instructions with regard to judging others is very simply put; He says, "Don't." The average Christian is the most piercingly critical individual known. Criticism is one of the ordinary activities of people, but in the spiritual realm nothing is accomplished by it. The effect of criticism is the dividing up of the strengths of the one being criticized. The Holy Spirit is the only one in the proper position to criticize, and He alone is able to show what is wrong without hurting and wounding.
>
> It is impossible to enter into fellowship with God when you are in a critical mood. Criticism serves to make you harsh, vindictive, and cruel, and leaves you with the soothing and flattering idea that you are somehow superior to others. Jesus says that as His disciple you should cultivate a temperament that is never critical.[2]

In dealing with the principles of communication, the Bible cautions us against using our lips to defile. To defile means to deliberately make something unclean or impure. Worshipers must take care that their words encourage others toward righteousness rather than delighting in impurity or crudity. Jesus says this action flows from the abundance of the heart:

> The mouth speaks what the heart is full of. . . . These people honor me with their lips, but their hearts are far from me. . . . But the things that come out of a person's mouth come from the heart, and these defile them.
> —MATTHEW 12:34; 15:8, 18

The apostle James takes the application a step further. He contends that such behavior defiles the whole body:

> The tongue also is a fire, a world of evil among the parts of the body. It corrupts the whole body, sets the whole course of one's life on fire,

and is itself set on fire by hell. . . . But no human being can tame the tongue. It is a restless evil, full of deadly poison.

—JAMES 3:6, 8

Healthy Communication

There are four primary principles for healthy communication with others: delight, discernment, decisive determination, and discipline.

The writer of Ephesians tells us that when we talk, we should not say harmful things but say what people need. Our words should strengthen others. We need to make sure that what is said will do good for those we come in contact with so that they will listen to what we have to say (Eph 4:29).

Healthy Communication Is Delightful

Proverbs 27 calls the counsel coming from a friend sweet and delightful.

> Perfume and incense bring joy to the heart,
>   and the pleasantness of a friend
> springs from their heartfelt advice.
>   —PROVERBS 27:9

How do we experience this delight? Look how the psalmist suggest we receive it:

> My tongue will proclaim your righteousness,
>   your praises all day long.
>   —PSALM 35:28

Healthy Communication Is Discerning

For the worshiper, communication to those in partnership must be guided by discernment. Our communication with others should not be foolish or without tact and grace. This takes wisdom. Proverbs refers to the strength and danger of words: "The words of the reckless pierce like swords, but the tongue of the wise brings healing" (Prov 12:18), and "the tongue has the power of life and death, and those who love it will eat its fruit" (Prov 18:21).

Healthy Communication Is Decisive and Determined

Worshipers must be determined to speak truth and exalt the Lord with their words, even when it is difficult or people don't want to hear us:

> Our mouths were filled with laughter,
> our tongues with songs of joy.
> Then it was said among the nations,
> "The Lord has done great things for them."
> —PSALM 126:2

Guard your communication. No matter who you are speaking to, whether it's one person or an audience, seek to know and practice the wisdom of God. Ask God to help you learn how to guard and protect your heart according to Philippians 4:7: "And the peace of God, which surpasses all understanding, will guard your hearts and minds through Christ Jesus."

Healthy Communication Is Disciplined

Finally, discipline yourself to listen carefully, reflect on others' opinions, be open and friendly, practice honesty and confidence (not arrogance), speak softly and to the point, cultivate the ability to accept feedback with grace, keep an open mind, respect the other person's opinion, be empathic, and carefully guard your body language.[3]

Communication

But the wisdom that comes from heaven is first of all pure; then peace-loving, considerate, submissive, full of mercy and good fruit, impartial and sincere. Peacemakers who sow in peace reap a harvest of righteousness.

—JAMES 3:17–18

CHAPTER 23

CONFIDENCE

"Does he ever get afraid?" I asked Anastasia about our guide while we were relaxing on the bank after lunch.

"He's pretty confident," she replied.

"I would like to know that kind of confidence for a day," I replied, half joking.

"He does hate snakes. An encounter with a snake will get him going. But in general, he is not a fearful guy."

"I was scared of my own shadow growing up. It doesn't control me now, but confidence doesn't just come naturally for me."

"I haven't always been confident," John said as he walked past us. I followed him. "So where . . . when did you find it?"

He kept moving. "I think confidence comes from knowing who you are and what you put your confidence in." I needed more. "So what does that mean for you?" I questioned again.

"I was made for the river, plain and simple. Once I embraced that, the outside couldn't tell me who I was. I'm anchored. It keeps things clear for me. For a while I tried to let circumstances or people define me. Not anymore. True confidence comes from knowing who you are."

Neal overheard and chimed in. "So existential, boys. I know who I am! A New Yorker in the friggin' wilderness trying to figure out how I got here."

I mulled over what John said. He stopped, turned, and faced me and put his finger on my chest. "It's in here."

I didn't respond. He paused awkwardly before he continued. "Nothing else will give you your sense of self. It has to come from within. You don't get it from your career, a person, or a full bank account. If you don't know who you are, you'll spend your whole life chasing someone else's idea of who you should be. That's a sure-fire way into the arms of fear. Once you sort out your identity, you find your confidence, plain and simple."

"So back to my original question to Anastasia: Are you ever afraid?"

His next statement connected with me deeply. "Why should I be? As long as I'm in the river, what else is there?"

The LORD is my light and my salvation—
    whom shall I fear?
The LORD is the stronghold of my life—
    of whom shall I be afraid?
When the wicked advance against me
    to devour me,
it is my enemies and my foes
    who will stumble and fall.
Though an army besiege me,
    my heart will not fear;
though war break out against me,
    even then I will be confident.

—PSALM 27:1–3

Confidence comes from knowing our identity. It comes from knowing you didn't make yourself, and you don't need the perfect plan for your life. Confidence comes from knowing that we didn't come up with this whole thing; God did. Our confidence is not in what we can be or do but who God is and what he has done. Our confidence rests on the foundation that God made everything. God made us, and because of Jesus, we are children of God. From that basis we live, love, and learn. We prepare. We gather knowledge and wisdom knowing that by his Spirit and Word, we will have all that we need to accomplish his purposes for us.

> See what great love the Father has lavished on us, that we should be called children of God! And that is what we are! The reason the world does not know us is that it did not know him. Dear friends, now we are children of God, and what we will be has not yet been made known. But we know that when Christ appears, we shall be like him, for we shall see him as he is.
> —1 JOHN 3:1–2

Because we are in Christ Jesus, there is nothing to fear! The more we immerse ourselves in the river that is the Lord, we find life and freedom from shame and people pleasing. We find worthiness and identity based on who he says we are, not in who we feel we are. The way of worship is placing our confidence in Jesus.

As artists and leaders, we look for confidence in our gifting or chase significance in things that we can lose. We allow our confidence and identity to ride on the rollercoaster of feelings. We ride the same route over and over—around and around we go. We dwell on old wounds, past mistakes, childhood trauma, or neglect and desperately try to make sense of it. We become controlled by the pursuit of approval or the frenetic pursuit of power and comfort.

Those lesser gods we unwittingly worship will destroy us and distort our lives. They will disappoint us in every way. We will continually be more and more fearful because the idol we have constructed is not trustworthy. To paraphrase Tim Keller, if we fail those idols, they will never forgive us. The way of worship beckons us to return to the river and return to Jesus, who says, "I am the living water."

Many years ago, I found myself far down the wayward path of finding my identity and significance in lesser things. Slowly but surely, I had fashioned an idol to bow down to: the idol of achievement. In the name of Christian ministry, I had placed much of my significance in what I could achieve and in the approval of others. I was a hardworking songwriter and a worship pastor at one of the largest churches in America. I was about to sign a worldwide record contract. I seemed to be at the peak of success. Then, at the last minute, that contract opportunity went away due to a change in the company's leadership, and I came face to face with the devastation of resting my identity in lesser things. When the contract collapsed, so did my view of myself. My joy left. Fear took over. Since the new executives didn't see my songs and talent as worthy, I internalized the message that I was unworthy.

By his great mercy, the Spirit of God met me in that wallowing. He pulled me up into his arms and reminded me who I was and to whom I belonged. I wasn't what anyone else said about me. I was a cherished, one-of-a-kind child of God. I would never go back to lesser things. Being a child of the Most High is my identity. He is my confidence.

When people use the word *confidence*, they often picture self-assurance, poise, self-reliance, coolness, and certainty. For many, confidence means an attitude of "I've got this figured out." It could mean faith in oneself and one's powers without any suggestion of conceit or arrogance. This is especially true when a person can demonstrate long years (maybe hundreds of hours) of experience.

Most "formal" definitions place a great emphasis on one's own ability to succeed or belief in achieving a goal. But to those of us called to be worshipers of the Most High God, our total confidence must be in the Lord. By nature, our understanding of confidence must be oriented in a different direction. Only Jesus can place in a our heart that quiet assurance that we are capable, because we no longer have to believe that *we* are enough—only that *he* is enough.

The psalmist says, "It is better to take refuge in the LORD than to trust in humans" (Ps 118:8).

While it may be tempting to place our confidence in our résumé, our skills, our network, our bank account, or our personality, the only true source of confidence is Jesus.

> In him and through faith in him we may approach God with freedom and confidence.
> —EPHESIANS 3:12

In the Greek New Testament, confidence is used thirty-one times in four unique ways. The most common use of "confidence" (*parrhēsía*) is a sense of boldness.[1] In worship, confidence is demonstrated when worshipers freely speak in an unreserved manner about the things of God. They are fearless and cheerful rather than afraid or self-conscious. Having confidence in Jesus allows the worship leader to focus on the higher goal of spiritual truth and formation instead of on his or her own image or safety.

This confidence from the Lord brings with it strength. God provides three basic resources through his strength: protection, peace, and purpose.

We can have confidence because we know God is protecting us. The Bible tells us that those who place their confidence in Christ will rest in his protection. He keeps "your foot from being snared," and his children have "a refuge":

For the LORD will be at your side
and will keep your foot from being snared.
—PROVERBS 3:26

Whoever fears the LORD has a secure fortress,
and for their children it will be a refuge.
—PROVERBS 14:26

This confidence in God's protection brings peace into the heart of the worshiper. The prophet Isaiah tells us that confidence is connected to quietness. In the quietness, God is your strength. God is gracious, exalted, and merciful, and he blesses all those that wait for him:

In quietness and trust is your strength . . .
Yet the Lord longs to be gracious to you;
therefore he will rise up to show you compassion.
For the Lord is a God of justice.
Blessed are all who wait for him!
—ISAIAH 30:15, 18

Once we can rest confidently in God's protection and peace, we can move forward, focused on our true purpose. God gives his vote of affirmation. He is the support for us, so the wisdom of God might be made known by the church. Those who worship him can and do find strength, encouragement, and rest of heart:

According to his eternal purpose that he accomplished in Christ Jesus our Lord. In him and through faith in him we may approach God with freedom and confidence. I ask you, therefore, not to be discouraged because of my sufferings for you, which are your glory.
—EPHESIANS 3:11–13

Ultimately, we can have confidence because we know that God will overcome evil, and our success comes from him. Nothing that rises against God will be successful in the end.

> You knew that you yourselves had better and lasting possessions. So do not throw away your confidence; it will be richly rewarded. You need to persevere so that when you have done the will of God, you will receive what he has promised.
> —HEBREWS 10:34–36

So, to the worshiper, Jesus is the source, strength, and success of our confidence. Our confidence is not found in a stronger self-image or self-assurance—it is found in Jesus. In the process, God may grant stronger self-esteem and self-confidence, but that renewed strength will find its source in the giver of all life and our great high priest, Jesus.

> Since we have a great high priest who has ascended into heaven . . . let us then approach God's throne of grace with confidence, so that we may receive mercy and find grace to help us in our time of need.
> —HEBREWS 4:14, 16

Once worshipers, and those leading worship, discover and understand that their true confidence is only found in Jesus, they can be assured that:

- He willingly hears our prayers and supplications.
- He joyfully joins us anytime we worship.
- He graciously serves as our great high priest.
- He forever keeps his promises.
- He gives spiritual power to those who seek him.
- He renews mercy every morning.

- He ever intercedes on our behalf.
- He serves as our own, personal worship leader.
- He genuinely protects and defends against the forces of evil.
- He teaches you and me how to lead worship.

This is the confidence we have in approaching God: that if we ask anything according to his will, he hears us.

—1 JOHN 5:14

At the end of the day, when you and I are prepared to take on the mantle of worship leader, we will better understand how calling, character, competence, confidence, and courage fit into a much larger, greater, sovereign plan totally orchestrated by God. We will find that he shapes us as worshipers. You will understand how all confidence for doing ministry is found in the person of Jesus Christ, and you will discover how Jesus is the source, strength, and success for all confidence. The confidence he gives is eternal in scope.

Over the past many lessons, we have seen how being a worshiper of God requires us to pay attention to our hearts. In chapter 2, we dealt with the call to worship. Chapters 5–6 explored the principles of God's Spirit dwelling in the heart of each worshiper. In chapter 7, we learned that the cornerstone of a worshiping heart is a grateful spirit. Chapters 9–13 uncovered the deeper principles of character, brokenness, humility, and integrity. In chapters 18–20, we looked at how community must be cultivated through unity, service, sacrifice, and good communication. In this lesson, we've learned how our confidence as worship leaders must rest only on the work of Jesus. All of these subjects, in one way or another, help prepare the worshiper's heart for a lifetime's task of leading worship. In the next chapter, we will learn how nurturing (and paying attention to) all of these heart issues will enable and equip us to navigate through some of the most treacherous and challenging life lessons.

CHAPTER 24

NAVIGATION

"Left forward hard!" John commanded. Our raft swung sharply to the right.

"Forward hard!" All paddlers dug into the water in perfect unison, and we lurched forward, toward the right fork in the river. A rocky island covered with trees divided the waters in two. The rapids were playfully bouncy as we navigated around.

"We call that J and H Island," John said as we swiftly passed by. The river descended steadily over about five-hundred yards until the two branches joined again on the downriver side of the island.

As the rapids calmed down, I wanted to get the story.

"J and H?" I asked.

"Jekyll and Hyde," Anastasia replied.

"So you're not sure what you're going to get?" Leah asked.

"Exactly," John replied.

"Why does it keep you guessing?" I wanted to know.

"It's not about guessing. You have to do your homework. Depending on the weather, the CFS, and the canyon wall activity, either side can be happy or mean. It's important to know what you're getting into. Last year on a high-water day in mid-June, a large boulder had tumbled in the middle of the night, and the water was so high you couldn't see it. It presented some nasty problems for some unprepared paddlers."

"So you guys have to scout it out then?"

"Always."

"What does CFS mean?"

"Cubic feet per second. It's how we measure water flow."

"So how do you remember all this stuff?" I asked.

John reached into his dry bag and tossed me a small, leather-bound notebook.

"That's how. Take a look. Just go to the last page that has my scribbling on it," he said.

I thumbed through. Nearly every page was full of notes and sketches. When I got to the last few pages, today's date was on the top of the left side followed by two-and-a-half pages of notes, directions, arrows, and drawings. Things like *Technical and slow at rainbow* or *Right side at J & H*.

"This is really cool. You do this for every trip?"

"Absolutely. It's how I navigate. You have to plan. You have to chart your course. You have to pay attention to what the river is saying. The guides share information from day to day, we scout early in the morning, we make our plan, and then we execute. You know what Ben Franklin said, right?"

"I'm not sure. What?"

"By failing to prepare, you are preparing to fail. That's strong, isn't it? The reality is, sometimes you have to make last-minute adjustments. You can't mitigate all risk, but if you have a foundational preparation, you will navigate well. The stakes are too high not to."

You are my portion, LORD;
> I have promised to obey your words.
> I have sought your face with all my heart;
>> be gracious to me according to your promise.
> I have considered my ways
>> and have turned my steps to your statutes.
> I will hasten and not delay
>> to obey your commands.
>> —PSALM 119:57–60

Navigation means charting a course. To navigate well, we must see what lies ahead, identify obstacles, and determine the safest and most beautiful way to go. Navigating well requires intentionality. A navigator will know their position at all times relative to where they are coming from and where they are going. A great navigator must be aware of current conditions. With relentless intention, a great navigator will chart a course based on position, desired destination, and the conditions of any given route to traverse safely. It requires planning. It requires thought and intention.

The psalmist declares in Psalm 119, "I have considered my ways [current position] and have turned my steps to your statutes [desired destination]." John knew the importance of course charting, planning, and navigating safely. He consulted the wisdom of other guides, scouted the water before our run, and made notes to remind himself of the trouble spots to avoid, the best way to approach any given rapid, and the direction to take when options abounded. He didn't leave it to chance. He didn't enter into the trip with anything but fierce and wise preparation.

This is just as important for the way of worship, both in self-leadership and leadership of others. To run the waters of life with

Jesus and to live a life of worship is to intentionally chart our course according to his Word and his way. To be victorious in our spiritual battle, we must be vigilant, allowing the Holy Spirit to speak through his statutes; stay constantly in his Word; and pray and meditate for his sanctifying work to be done in us.

This is true not only of the inward work of the Spirit but also the outward work of our hands. It is vital to help our "rafters"—our teams and parishioners—navigate safely. We are making plans for the betterment of our ministry culture, casting a vision of a beautiful future, and creating worship environments to bring our people to the table of the Lord. This demands diligent work in charting our course daily, weekly, seasonally, and yearly. Just like our raft would not just drift toward the safest rapid without careful guidance, our worship services and discipleship culture will not drift toward excellence. It takes wisdom, diligence, and intentionality. The way of worship calls us to be thorough and excellent navigators.

> He pointed out to him the bearings of the coast, explained to him the variations of the compass, and taught him to read in that vast book opened over our heads which they call heaven, and where God writes in azure with letters of diamonds.
> —ALEXANDRE DUMAS, *THE COUNT OF MONTE CRISTO*

Our son, Jeremy, is a pilot, and he loves to fly. He is skilled, careful, and safe. I love getting into his plane and flying from our home in south-central Virginia to Nashville, Tennessee. (His mother doesn't always enjoy it so much!)

Whenever Jeremy takes any kind of journey in his plane—in addition to checking the fuel level, tires, and mechanical condition of the aircraft—there are two things he always does before getting into the aircraft. First, he thoroughly checks the weather conditions, and second, he files a flight plan.

Pilots using Instrumental Flight Rules (IFR), electronic navigation instruments and systems to assist them in their journey, are required by the Federal Aviation Agency to file a flight plan listing time of departure, estimated air speed and altitude, route, and arrival time to the destination. Usually—especially when taking a longer trip—Jeremy engages the "automatic pilot" system. Autopilot tracks his speed, bearing, altitude, direction, trip distance, sunrise and sunset time (and a whole lot more) for the journey. It is equipped with a special type of GPS that, when properly programed, can guide the plane safely to its destination.

GPS is a truly amazing system that uses at least twenty-four satellites. Originally designed by the U.S. Department of Defense and made available for civilian use in the early 1980s, GPS works in any weather condition, anywhere in the world, twenty-four hours a day.[1] People all over the world use GPS to help them operate aircraft, automobiles, buses, trucks, and ships. We use them to measure running or walking routes, map golf courses, track cell phone location, and more. It takes wisdom, diligence, and intentionality to properly use a GPS, and you have to pay attention to its guidance in order to successfully and safely arrive at your destination.

The worshiper has a type of GPS implanted deep inside his or her heart: the Holy Spirit. Once the worshiper and the Holy Spirit unite, God begins establishing gifts, talents, and desires—guiding them in his plan for their lives. As the worshiper obeys the promptings of the Holy Spirit, God begins to guide, direct, and lead so that his purposes are fulfilled. King David, king of Israel and worshiper of the most high God, reminds us, "The plans of the LORD stand firm forever, the purposes of His heart through all generations" (Ps 33:11).

God, through the Holy Spirit's ministry to the worshiper, begins to prompt, counsel, and equip. Soon, God's plans really start becoming the worshiper's desires and ambitions. King David's son, Solomon, one of the wisest men to ever live, wrote this in Proverbs 19: "Many are the plans in a person's heart, but it is the LORD's purpose that prevails." (Prov 19:21).

King Solomon also penned a formula for being successful in life with the assurance of receiving God's blessing and direction:

> Trust in the Lord with all your heart
>> and lean not on your own understanding;
> in all your ways submit to him,
>> and he will make your paths straight.
>> —PROVERBS 3:5–6

How does this apply to the way of worship? How does God help us navigate the challenges we face every day?

You must let this truth settle deep into your heart: God has a plan for your life! Perhaps the most familiar passage of Scripture teaching this principle is found in Jeremiah 29:11–14. While the original message was addressed to the Judean exiles coming from Jerusalem to Babylon, its teaching about God's treatment for those who trust in him is still appropriate today. In Jeremiah 29:10, the prophet writes to tell the exiles that one day they will return to Jerusalem (after seventy years). Verse 11 reassures these Jewish people being taken into slavery that God has not forsaken them and that they will be restored:

> "For I know the plans I have for you," declares the LORD, "plans to prosper you and not to harm you, plans to give you hope and a future. Then you will call on me and come and pray to me, and I will listen to you. You will seek me and find me when you seek me with all your heart. I will be found by you."
>> —JEREMIAH 29:11–14

David Guzik explains, "If by quoting Jeremiah 29:11 we are thinking of our security in Christ, then the wording is appropriate, even if the historical context does not apply."[2] From this verse, we can come to understand a few principles.

God's GPS is always on track (Jer 29:11). God knows the plans he has for those that love him and are called according to his purposes (Rom 8:28–35).

God's provisions are certain. God's plans are for you, personally! His relationship is personal. He wants you and me to prosper. He is the God of hope. The God you worship has already, before the foundation of the world, planned a future for you that is fulfilling and meaningful.

You can trust not only God's ultimate plan but also the process he takes to get there. It is easy to want to take shortcuts to where you think God wants you to go. But just as he instructed Jeremiah to tell the chosen people of Israel to "Call upon me, pray, and seek," you must follow his map, his GPS, his strategy.

God's promise endures forever. If you and I call upon him, pray to, and seek him, he will listen, and he will make himself available. He can be found by you!

God desires to use you and me to fulfill his purposes. This is the important thing to remember. God really wants your joy to be full. John, the apostle, said as much in his first epistle: "And these things we write to you that your joy may be full." The psalmist turns his song into a prayer: "May He grant you according to your heart's desire, And fulfill all your purpose (Ps 20:4 NKJV). The more you worship and seek God, the more he will reveal his purposes to you. The more you walk according to his purposes, the more joy you will receive.

God's plan and purpose are always successful for those submitting to his process. Any kind of growth or goal takes time. Remember, this process begins with humility. It means placing more significance on others than on yourself, and it means knowing the difference between self-confidence and pride—and living it!

Fulfilling God's purpose is a *calling and a process*. When God calls you and me to fulfill his purposes, he obligates himself to equip us. We can trust him to provide for us in every area. It is God who perfects, establishes, strengthens, and settles a person, a work, a ministry, or a mission, all for his glory and purposes and for the testimony of Jesus Christ.

God is the one who prepares us for the way of worship. In this book, we have discussed many ways that we can practice preparing our hearts for worship. But ultimately, our growth and sanctification is a work of God. The biblical examples of this are almost too numerous to count.

> In their hearts humans plan their course,
>> but the LORD establishes their steps.
>> —PROVERBS 16:9

> Many are the plans in a person's heart,
>> but it is the LORD's purpose that prevails.
>> —PROVERBS 19:21

> And we know that in all things God works for the good of those who love him, who have been called according to his purpose.
>> —ROMANS 8:28

> For God has put it into their hearts to accomplish his purpose . . . until God's words are fulfilled.
>> —REVELATION 17:17

Quickly read Psalm 1. In these six verses, the psalmist outlines the benefits of allowing God to become your navigator, guide, and leader:

1. **Separated from the world (v. 1).** God is preparing and teaching you how to resist the temptation of standing next to or sitting alongside of those actively engaged in evil.

2. **Satisfied by the Word (v. 2).** God is preparing and teaching you the joy of developing the discipline of twenty-four-hour meditation on his Word.

3. **Situated by the water (v. 3).** God is preparing and teaching you to enjoy being in his presence. Your life will yield fruit, your hunger for God will not wither, and whatever you do will prosper!

4. **Sustained by our worship (v. 6).** This is the benefit of genuine relationship: the Lord watches over the way of the righteous (Ps 1:6).

Now, you are ready! In the next chapter, we will explore what it means to have vision.

CHAPTER 25

VISION

"Are you guys ready to be transported?" John asked.

"You bettah have a powerful transportah if ya gonna carry this Brooklyn boy!" Neal quipped before anyone else could answer.

"When we round this bend, you'll see what I mean," the guide said, chuckling.

The river opened up wide. We coasted into a spectacular view. Loud screeches echoed from overhead as three birds of prey circled high above the canyon.

"Wow, the red-tails are out today!" Anastasia commented.

Everyone took in the sight with delight. The azure sky was a brilliant canopy over the red rock canyon walls. The pine and spruce trees were mirrored in the placid waters. An occasional cloud floated slowly overhead, making dark, shaded shapes on the water like giant shadow puppets. A gentle breeze wafted through the canyon. We couldn't hear highway sounds. There was only beauty and peace. Everyone quieted their voices as if to not disturb the tranquility. It seemed sacred.

"A little different than the big city," I commented to Neal, who sat across the raft from me.

"Just a little," he said reverently.

"You're probably used to this view, aren't you?" Leah asked.

"I never get over it," John said as he craned his neck, peering around the canyon. "Beyond the terrestrial beauty of this place, I see more."

"What do you mean?" I asked as we floated. I felt very small in this majestic place.

"When I take people down the river, I really want them to see what I see and know what I know."

John had a way of communicating almost cryptically, forcing you to engage and ask more questions. He wouldn't just come out with it. He drew you in. It was frustrating and intriguing at the same time. It was certainly memorable.

"You want us to see the river differently or something?" I asked.

"I want you to see what's beyond the river. If you're awake to it, you won't be the same."

I was growing more impatient.

"Now I just feel dumb. What is it you want us to see?"

"In this moment, what are the most important things to you?" John asked.

I thought for a moment. "Leah, of course. My faith. My family."

"Beautiful," he said. "If you're anything like me, being out here, being in the river, has purified what is most important to you. Being in the river to me means not allowing my passions to be consumed by lesser things. My hope is people will go back to their everyday lives with a renewed sense of the proper order of things. A renewed resolve that they are chasing the right things. Not money, comfort, or notoriety, but something far greater. Faith, hope, and love. Generously giving themselves away to care, lift up, and heal."

"Easier said than done. Life is so busy, I think sometimes you wake up and don't even realize your priorities have shifted. They are nearly upside down." Franny surprised us with her thoughtfulness.

I finally got it. In experiencing the purity and beauty of the river, if we looked for it, we could see ourselves and what we truly hope for more clearly. We could see the leanings of our hearts more clearly in the wild. John's last statement finally answered my question.

"There's a better way. *That* is what I want people to see."

The Spirit of the Sovereign LORD is on me,
    because the LORD has anointed me
    to proclaim good news to the poor.
He has sent me to bind up the brokenhearted,
    to proclaim freedom for the captives
    and release from darkness for the prisoners,
to proclaim the year of the LORD's favor
    and the day of vengeance of our God,
to comfort all who mourn,
    and provide for those who grieve in Zion—
to bestow on them a crown of beauty
    instead of ashes,
the oil of joy
    instead of mourning,
and a garment of praise
    instead of a spirit of despair.
They will be called oaks of righteousness,
    a planting of the LORD
    for the display of his splendor.

—ISAIAH 61:1–3

The way of worship calls us to a place of vision, seeing what others do not see and guiding them so that vision catches fire in their spiritual eyes. This kind of vision is prophetic in nature: we must learn to see clearly what is happening around us. We must identify the idols that we tend to fashion and call for their destruction. We must illuminate the hope of what is to come, the kingdom of heaven.

> In the Old Testament, two words are used to describe the prophet. The earlier of the two is the word *ro'eh*, which roughly means, "the one who sees." Later, the more common word used for a prophet is *nabi*, which can be loosely translated as, "the one who speaks," particularly, on behalf of another. A prophet is one who sees a different world, and says a different word.
>
> —DR. GLENN PACKIAM[1]

In any role, it is easy for the tyranny of what is urgent to keep our eyes fixed on what is right in front of us. We get in the habit of prioritizing what is efficient and productive. We slide into the rhythms of the calendar, programs, and liturgies. Sundays keep coming, one after the other, and we prepare environments and creative offerings to worship God in the sanctuary. Just like Franny in our story, we can wake up one day and realize our priorities have shifted, we are upside down, and we have lost the artistic and prophetic edge God calls us to.

John wanted us to see a better way than the pursuit of lesser things. He wanted us to experience the river and then bring that renewed vision into everyday life.

To be prophetic in our worship leadership means calling for idols to be crushed, speaking the truth of where we are, and pointing to the great hope of what's to come. The way of worship by God's grace calls us to live this great mission through our art, our songs, our liturgies, and our lives.

The great mystery for the worshiper is that our vision—our great mission—is focused on one person: Jesus. The way of worship calls us, by God's grace, to live this great vision through our art, our songs, our liturgies, and our lives.

Vision begins by knowing an organization's purpose, values, and goal. The purpose defines the group's reason for existence. Most companies will have a "vision statement," list of "core values," or "company tenets" to help guide decision making and daily operations, policy, deportment, and conduct. Vision helps everyone stay focused on what is most important and not get lost or bogged down by the details.

This goal crafts a vision that can be clearly imagined and articulated. A vision statement can be written as a one-sentence declaration that clearly defines the short-term (and often long-term) goals and objectives. Having a vision to guide an organization's everyday decisions is important on both the personal and professional levels.

Personal Vision

To the worshiper, establishing a personal vision (and perhaps even a mission statement) may help in identifying individual core values and calling. It establishes a paradigm within which you can grow in character, holiness, honesty, and an authentic way of leading worship. Clearly articulated and internalized vision provides the strength to live according to a biblical vision above the cross-current pressures of culture.

In Luke 4, we read the account of Jesus in Nazareth, the community in which he had been raised. He goes into the synagogue on the Sabbath day and stands up to read. He is handed the book of the prophet Isaiah. When he opens the book, he finds the place where his very own "personal vision statement" is written:

The Spirit of the Lord is on me,
> because he has anointed me
> to proclaim good news to the poor.
He has sent me to proclaim freedom for the prisoners
> and recovery of sight for the blind,
to set the oppressed free,
> to proclaim the year of the Lord's favor.

—LUKE 4:18–19

When Jesus finished, he rolled up the scroll, gave it back to the attendant, and sat down. Everyone in the building was watching Jesus as he announced, "Today this scripture is fulfilled in your hearing." It is important to note that "all in the building spoke well of Jesus and were amazed at the gracious words that came from his lips." That day, Jesus revealed his life vision and purposes.

In this moment, he proclaims he is anointed to preach the gospel, explains and proclaims his plan to heal the brokenhearted, proclaim liberty, and give new sight to the blind. He demonstrates a holy disposition, conduct, and graciousness at a level never before heard or seen by the world.

That day, Jesus demonstrated how a life can be based on and lived according to a biblical vision. He had a clear vision of his calling, with whom he was to fulfill that vision, when the vision was to be revealed, and how that vision was to be accomplished.

What does it mean for a worshiper to live a life based on biblical vision?

Biblical vision is informed by the person and promises of God. The worshiper's vision is based and built upon an ever-deepening relationship with one person: Jesus. This kind of vision-relationship provides the worshiper an opportunity to establish parameters for communicating personal and professional direction.

Biblical vision is motivated by a genuine desire to please God and serve people. Worshipers gratefully assume the role of servant leader.

Whatever they do, they work at it with all of their heart as unto the Lord and not for men. They believe they are serving Christ as they serve others.

Biblical vision is inspired by a set of core values that reflect the purposes of God. Plans are realized according to God's purposes (Prov 19:21). The worshiper can then lead, imagine, and mentor according to the scope of his or her vision.

Biblical vision is enriched by relationships—with God and with others! Worship is relational. It involves the upward relationship that is totally God-focused as well as the horizonal relationship with fellow worshipers, brothers, and sisters.

Biblical vision is empowered by the Spirit of God so that we can see, do, believe in, and reach for what seems impossible. Holy Spirit-led vision provides opportunity and prompting for the worshiper to aim higher. The things to which they commit themselves will more clearly reflect a strong commitment to a sovereign God. Stewardship of God's resources begins to take on a more meaningful purpose.

Biblical vision is recognized in those who realize they are part of something bigger than themselves. Such vision provides a platform for the worshiper to strive, thrive, and come alive in Christ.

It is essential for the worshiper to know how to identify and cultivate personal vision. In so doing, they will more freely imagine and implement future dreams and ideals. They can better "capture a vision of the big picture" for themselves and their organizations or groups. And they can help develop strategy for accomplishing what they know they and their organizations have been called to do.

Professional Vision

A professional vision establishes a platform for accountability, nurturing the anointing process, and developing a spirit of affirmation among the team members. Those who intentionally identify their professional vision are able to engage others around it, inspire with confidence, and motivate their team to make more meaningful decisions. Their commitment is to keeping their priorities straight and living by a commitment to and love for what matters most: Jesus.

When worshipers are intentional about their purposes, their operational scope grows, develops, and matures. They begin asking the "What's next?" question. When the worshiper learns to see potential (personal and professional), they can inspire others to press on until their vision and purposes are achieved. When worshipers internalize their vision, they will live in a way that reflects those values, especially in how relationships are established and nurtured. The worship leader must be intentional in identifying a vision, communicating it to the rest of their team and reflecting it in their own lifestyle.

Worshipers taking on the role of a visionary leader will naturally learn to choose eternal gain over instant gratification. It is when they refuse to allow their own self-serving interests to distort their vision of Jesus—when Jesus becomes their vision—that they enjoy the benefit of Holy Spirit-led wisdom, victory in spiritual battle, dignity, delight in serving, shelter, inheritance, and treasure. So much so that the old Irish hymn becomes their theme:

> Be thou my vision, O Lord of my heart;
> naught be all else to me, save that thou art—
> thou my best thought by day or by night,
> waking or sleeping, thy presence my light. . . .
> High King of heaven, my victory won,
> may I reach heaven's joys, O bright heav'n's Sun!
> Heart of my own heart, whatever befall,
> still be my vision, O Ruler of all.[2]

CHAPTER 26

COLLABORATION

"Little John, come in. Little John, you there? Over. Little John, come in. You at the put-in yet? Over."

The garbled transmission sounded from near John's feet in the raft just as we left the shore and started our journey that morning.

John reached for his dry bag and pulled out a dingy yellow walkie-talkie.

"Already in. Going to be a fun run, Eighty-Four. Over."

"Roger that. Early bird today. I like it. I'm thirty or so ahead and through the boulder garden number one. Running high and smooth. I'll shout if there are any surprises, but looking good so far. Over."

"Copy that. Catch ya soon, Eighty-Four. Over and out."

John put the walkie-talkie back in his bag, pulled out a stick of sunblock, and started applying it to his nose.

"Eighty-Four? Is that his name?" I asked.

"Nickname."

"Does he work for you guys?"

"No, he's a great friend and mentor-guide for another outfit. There are several guiding companies in the area, but most of us that have been doing it a while are part of a collective. We take turns scouting for each other. Lots of incredible friendships have been formed in that group."

"That seems rare, given that you guys are competitors in business, right?"

"I guess so. There are a few that don't want to be a part of it. They would rather go it alone and separate out. They are missing out, though."

"What does it look like to be in the collective?" I asked. As a young leader, John's life intrigued me on so many levels.

"We meet for a breakfast every other week. We keep in touch with one another. Check on each other's families. We give out tongue-in-cheek awards at the end of the season. We scout for each other on the river. Do trainings together. We make each other better. It's great. My father started the guide collective over twenty years ago. I'm convinced that when you do things together, life is richer, you have support, and it's just more fun. Early in my career I thought I had to charge the hill on my own. Not anymore. We weren't meant to go it alone. Eighty-Four is one of my closest friends, and we met through the collective."

John's passion for the collective was evident. His love for his friends was inspiring.

"Okay, so Little John and Eighty-Four? Where did that come from?" Leah asked.

"Oh, that goes way back. I'm not sure that's important," John said as he grinned.

"Out with it, Little John. Let's have it!" Neal exclaimed.

"When I was in grade school, I was very small in stature, but my Dad said I had the heart of a lion, like Robin Hood's partner, Little John. He said that I was feisty and strong-willed but fiercely loyal. As an adult guide, he called me that one day in front of my guiding buddies, and it stuck. As for Eighty-Four, that's Jimmy. We call him Eighty-Four as in 1984, because he is stuck in eighties fashion.

Feathers his hair, comb in the back pocket, pulls up his tube socks, and wears his old cropped fishnet jersey from high school sometimes. He owns it, and it's hilarious. That's what makes the collective great— none of us are alike, but we all love and root for each other."

Two are better than one,
>because they have a good return for their labor:
If either of them falls down,
>one can help the other up.
But pity anyone who falls
>and has no one to help them up.
Also, if two lie down together, they will keep warm.
>But how can one keep warm alone?
Though one may be overpowered,
>two can defend themselves.
A cord of three strands is not quickly broken.
>—ECCLESIASTES 4:9–12

Collaboration is foundational in the way of worship. The more we collaborate with others, the less self-absorbed we become. We get different facets of God at work among us. We are not meant to go it alone. Working with others effectively shapes our faith and how it is fleshed out in the world around us. When we work together, when we trust each other, when the friction of our unique personalities knocks the rough edge's off of one another, we are better, stronger, safer, and more whole.

There is a tendency in life and leadership to ascend the mountain of life and work alone. This is a tool of the enemy. When we are isolated, we are weaker, vulnerable to attack, and limited in our perspective.

John, our guide, found great joy in connecting with his fellow guides. Even though they all worked for different rafting companies and were competing for the same customers, they realized they all win personally and professionally if they look after each other. This is so counterintuitive in today's me-oriented, win-at-all-costs culture. They developed peer-to-peer, lifelong relationships. They lifted one another up and looked out for the safety and welfare of the other members. Their businesses and lives thrived because of it. They were spared from needless tragedies on the water, and they were able to share experiences together, which made everything more enjoyable. When John and Jimmy exchanged messages over that walkie-talkie, it gave us all a window into the bigger picture. You could see the joy on John's face after hearing from his friend. It brought him joy to know that someone was out in front scouting possible pitfalls, and that they could share the joys of the river together.

As we guide our teams and parishioners in worship, it is critical that we reach out to others, support and be supported, teach and be taught, love and be loved. I found out later in our rafting trip that we actually had a follow spotter as well, a kayaker who came down the river behind us in case of emergency. Co-laborers in front, behind, and beside, navigating the river together: this is the way it should be. In short, when we collaborate, we are stronger, safer, and better, and we see more of the heart of God in each other and in our work.

The demands of our schedules will drag us toward busyness and isolation. Make it a priority to collaborate. In producing events, leading teams, writing music, crafting experiences, and even in writing this book with my friend Vernon, I have learned that collaborating is the way of worship. Collaborating is God's way, for he saw fit to allow us to collaborate in sharing the greatest story of all: his love for us.

Collaboration is at the heart of successful teamwork. To collaborate means "to work jointly with others or together, especially in an intellectual endeavor."[1]

While the words *collaboration, teamwork,* or *partnerships* never appear in the Bible, the principles for healthy relationship in any one of these capacities abound. Collaboration means people with different skill-sets work together to make something happen or solve a problem. Collaboration relies on healthy communication, cooperation, coordination, and teamwork. *Partnership* is an even stronger word, indicating that two people are co-laborers in the same important task.

In worship, a person can collaborate without developing a partnership, but a partnership will never function without collaborating. Perhaps the words of Proverbs 27:17 puts the principles of collaboration into perspective: "As iron sharpens iron, so one person sharpens another."

Collaboration with Unity

We discussed unity earlier in this book, and it is a key aspect of collaboration. Before you can collaborate with other people, you must establish a common purpose and goal, trusting each other, clarifying roles from the very beginning, and valuing diverse organizational, administrative, and communication skills within the group. This practice will unify the entire worship community, pastoral ministry, praise team, staff, and broader congregation. No leader works in a vacuum; they must have partners who catch the vision. The prophet Amos asks the question, "Do two people walk hand in hand if they aren't going to the same place?" (Amos 3:3 MSG). The writer of Ephesians provides perspective:

Live a life worthy of the calling you have received. Be completely humble and gentle; be patient, bearing with one another in love. Make every effort to keep *the unity of the Spirit through the bond of peace.*

—EPHESIANS 4:1–3; EMPHASIS ADDED

Collaboration according to Individual Gifts

The Bible teaches that Christ gives gifts for the edification of his body, the church. As worshipers collaborate with one another, their individual gifts come together for greater, richer, and more extensive ministry.

> But to each one of us grace has been given as Christ apportioned it. . . . So that the body of Christ may be built up . . . from him the whole body . . . grows and builds itself up in love, as each part does its work.
>
> —EPHESIANS 4:7, 12, 16

Worshipers must lean into this promise and build collaborative partnerships to strengthen the entire body. It only takes the unified work of two, three, or four worshipers operating with a spirit of grace and a heart for service for lives to be changed and much accomplished for the glory of God.

Collaboration in Ministry

In the New Testament, there are scores of examples where multiple people collaborate to see more things accomplished for the kingdom of God than would have been possible if any individual had worked alone. In Philippians 2, the apostle Paul refers to his "son in the ministry," Timothy, as being like-minded and genuine in his concern for the people of Philippi. They were unified in purpose. Paul commends Timothy for his proven character and willingness to minister as a partner sharing the gospel of Jesus Christ. The people at Philippi were fellow soldiers, collaborators, co-campaigners, associates in work, companions in labor, co-laborers, team members, helpers, and work fellows. The writer of Hebrews extends this principle by setting forth guidelines when collaborating with faithful partners in ministry:

And let us consider how we may spur one another on toward love
and good deeds . . . encouraging one another—and all the more as
you see the Day approaching.

—HEBREWS 10:24–25

Collaboration in Service

Paul also had a second person who worked with him in collaboration: Epaphroditus. Paul and Epaphroditus worked together as a team, and a closer look reveals the heart of this partnership. Paul calls Epaphroditus a brother (Phil 2:25) and companion in labor. There was a common bond—a relationship—between Paul and Epaphroditus that carried over into their servant-leadership role with the people with whom they collaborated. Epaphroditus had a genuine love for people, and they rejoiced when they saw him. They received him with gladness.

Even Jesus sent his disciples out in pairs to preach. God promises to be present when two or three join together. Two are to go to a brother when there has been a wrong. Partnerships are essential to the success of any ministry, especially worship ministries. When people work together, those involved have a sense of ownership in the task.

But worship leaders not only need to collaborate with their team members; they must also form a partnership with the other members of the congregation. Partnership in worship begins with the pastor and includes the staff, the various boards and committees, the congregation and the praise team, the worshiping community, and each individual musician.

Collaboration as a Family

One of the most important passages in the New Testament is the fulfillment of a prophecy in Joel 2:28. The apostle Peter quotes this verse when describing the Spirit of God being poured out upon all flesh. In the process, he gives an outline as to how the old and young are to work together to see the work of God accomplished. Jesus told his disciples to wait in Jerusalem until they are clothed with power from on high (Luke 24:49). He tells them that they will receive power when the Holy Spirit comes upon them, and "they will be His witnesses to the end of the world" (see Acts 1:8).

Jesus promises the disciples they will receive the "spirit of truth," and that when he comes, he will be their counselor (John 14:16). The apostle Peter explains this "coming of the Holy Spirit" by proclaiming Joel's prophecy:

> In the last days, God says,
> > I will pour out my Spirit on all people.
> Your sons and daughters will prophesy,
> > your young men will see visions,
> > your old men will dream dreams.
> > > —ACTS 2:17

There are four critical parts to this message: God pours out his Spirit upon all flesh; the sons and daughters will prophesy; the young will have visions; and the old will dream dreams. This verse is especially important for the worshiper, young and old alike. Notice that the Word of the Lord reads: "Your young men will see visions and your old men shall dream dreams."

There is an important emphasis on using the young and old together, in collaboration with one another. The Holy Spirit draws men and women, boys and girls, servants and leaders, lower and upper class, old and young together into unified ministry. This is not the spirit of a few select people who isolate themselves from parts of the body of Christ. This is the spirit of unity, and he empowers them to collaborate in meeting the needs of the body of Christ. When they do, they are empowered to walk by the Spirit, be led by the Spirit, worship in the Spirit, and exemplify the fruits of the Spirit.

Collaboration as a Team

Teamwork in worship is about much more than completing a task. It involves motivating people to collaborate together effectively for the purpose of a much higher goal: leading God's people in heartfelt worship. The strength of the team comes from each person supporting the others, communicating well, coordinating ideas without an agenda, and everyone putting their hand to the plow and sharing in partnership on every level.

Collaboration for the worship leader is more about facilitating the body of Christ in honest, heartfelt worship than it is about making decisions regarding stylistic preference, presentation, or performance. In the process, the worshiper develops a team that works toward realistic goals, single-minded priorities, and unified purpose. In developing the skill of collaboration, the worship leader will need to continually focus on consistent communication with the team, develop a heart for tolerance of other ideas, be willing to compromise, be authentic, work at developing teamwork, demonstrate consistency, and be reliable as a creative leader.[2] At the end of the day, collaboration gives the worshiper opportunity to join together many members with varying gifts for the glory of God and testimony of Jesus Christ.

> For just as each of us has one body with many members, and these members do not all have the same function, so in Christ we, though many, form one body, and each member belongs to all the others. We have different gifts, according to the grace given to each of us.
>
> —ROMANS 12:4–6

CHAPTER 27

PERSEVERING

"The last big one of the day is just ahead, and it's a fun one!" John exclaimed.

"What's this one called, 'drown the fat guy' or 'city boy suckah'?" Neal asked with a straight face.

It wasn't just what he said, it was how he said it that had us all in stitches. It was late afternoon, nearly dusk, and I found myself lamenting the idea of this trip ending. The beauty, the adventure, the new friends, the wildlife, the danger, the many facets of the river—it was unforgettable.

"That's hilarious, Neal! I may use one of those in the future. This one is actually called 'Chain-breaker Falls,'" John said.

"What's behind that name?" Leah asked.

"It had that name long before we got here. My dad told me it's because once you make it through, you realize there's nothing that can hold you back. You get a sense that you can accomplish anything. You're home free. Okay, lock in everyone, here we go! Forward hard!"

We secured our feet under the tubes of the raft and paddled with deep, long strokes as the water accelerated. Down and up through huge waves of whitewater we splashed. The frigid water poured over the front of the vessel with each rapid. Shouts of glee after each successfully navigated wave rang from our group. Once we cleared the final section, we hoisted our paddles in the air and smacked them together for a high-five. It was pure joy.

"I'm proud of you guys! What a great trip," John said as he pulled down the top of his wetsuit, revealing his muscled torso in a tight tank top of sorts. An elaborate tattoo blanketed his right shoulder. It was colorful intertwined roses and thorns. At the top, the name "Jenna Mae" was written in intricate calligraphy, and at the bottom were the words "Forward Hard."

"Awesome tat, man," I said.

"Thanks."

"I've been wanting to get one, but I don't think I have the arms for it." I flexed to get a laugh.

"Is Jenna Mae your lucky lady?" Franny asked.

I cringed at what might be an awkward moment, but John took it in stride.

"No, not so lucky. I actually have this tattoo for a couple of reasons. The first is to create something beautiful out of a nasty scar, and the second is to remember Jenna Mae, my mom. She passed when I was twelve after a long fight with cancer."

None of us knew what to say.

"I lost my mom early too," Neal said.

"Can't get away from suffering, can you? That was her phrase. She was an amazing lady. Whenever things got difficult, she would say, 'Forward hard.'" He looked down at the ink. "Suffering makes you real and makes you feel. Beauty is coming, but you've got to paddle through. Forward hard."

"I like that," Neal said. "Life isn't easy, but if you keep paddling, there's something amazing coming down the river."

"Well said, my friend. That's why I'll never stop running the river. I never take things for granted anymore. My grandma used to say, 'The river holds our tears and carries us through the canyon, and that is what love looks like.'"

Not only so, but we also glory in our sufferings, because we know that suffering produces perseverance; perseverance, character; and character, hope. And hope does not put us to shame, because God's love has been poured out into our hearts through the Holy Spirit, who has been given to us.

—ROMANS 5:3–5

The way of worship is fraught with resistance, adversity, and even suffering. Pain and heartache come to us all. No one is exempt. There will be times when you want to throw in the towel. There will be times when you wonder if it's worth it. Remember, when Jesus invites us to follow him, it comes with the instruction to "take up your cross." It's going to be more difficult than we dared imagine. It is going to be dangerous and full of struggle. The enemy will bombard us with every sort of attack. There will be hardship. There will be pain. But we have hope because we know suffering never has the final word.

God did not give himself a pass. He entered our suffering all the way until it killed him. He became the suffering servant and showed us a love that is not of this world. Jesus himself takes the brutal suffering of his torturous death on the cross and turns it into the greatest victory in history: our redemption! He persevered, and by his grace and power, we can too.

John's remembrance of his mother's love, and his perseverance in the wake of that tragic loss, was inspiring. John had discovered that enduring through difficulty is where the most rich and beautiful experiences are found. In persevering through pain, we experience the power and presence of God in deep and profound ways. In our perseverance, we reflect the hope that we have to the world. Our perseverance says, "Our God is with us, he is working all things for our good and his glory, and we have ultimate future glory with him." Persevering is not ignoring that things can be bad, even horrifying. Persevering is walking through it to the other side. We may bear the scars, but we will see salvation.

When he quoted his grandmother saying, "The river holds our tears and carries us through the canyon, and that is what love looks like," it shouted to me what our God does for us. His grace and love will carry us through the darkest of times. He will give us the power to continue on to what is waiting for us on the other side. We must continue to create, lead, and plan in the work God has called us to do. When we feel like quitting because it's just too hard, we can take heart and rest in the river of God's grace. He will carry us through. Keep your paddle in the water. Forward hard.

Forward hard! Whatever phrase inspires you to press on through suffering, the way of worship calls for perseverance! What benefit is found in suffering for those that diligently seek to worship God in spirit and truth? There are four principles that may help all of us push through suffering and find hope when things get hard.

First, it is through suffering that the Holy Spirit refines our worship and teaches us some of life's greatest lessons. God uses suffering and brokenness to draw us to himself and to demonstrate his love to us in the most powerful way. He shows himself worthy of worship, the defender of the broken, and the one who lifts the heart and head to a place of satisfaction and joy. God often uses moments of suffering to reveal to us the most about himself. Paul tells us that "Suffering produces perseverance; perseverance, character; and character, hope" (Rom 5:3–4). The road to suffering teaches us endurance, develops integrity, and increases our faith.

Second, Jesus can be trusted even when you can't see or feel him. God uses suffering for his glory, and nothing done for his glory is ever wasted. Psalm 115:1 says, "Not to us, not to us but to your name be the glory, because of your love and faithfulness."

Many times during days of suffering, God moves through the circumstances, causing the most physical, emotional, and mental pain to ultimately calm our fears, settle our anxious spirit, speak peace, and fill our life with his presence. It is this presence that brings comfort. It is his presence that turns the torment of doubt and fear into a platform for praise, a testimony of purpose, and a tower of great hope.

Third, any suffering lasts only for a season. In writing to the church at Rome, the apostle Paul spoke great words of hope to the brothers and sisters immersed in, consumed by, and captive to the pressure that comes with persecution and great suffering:

> I consider that our present sufferings are not *worth comparing* with the glory that will be revealed in us. . . . But if we hope for what we do not yet have, *we wait for it patiently.*
> —ROMANS 8:18, 25; EMPHASIS ADDED

The antidote to the anxiety caused by suffering is "hope with perseverance" in the Lord. Centuries ago, Jeremiah the prophet wrote words of hope during a time when his strength had faded. He says, "There is hope!" He reinforces his conviction by saying, "There is great hope" and that the Lord's mercies are renewed every morning. He concludes his affirmation by giving testimony to the truth that God is faithful, the Lord is his portion, and because of that, "I have hope" (see Lam 3:21).

Fourth, God often uses suffering to draw us closer to himself and strengthen our relationship with him. Our relationship with God is at the heart of our worship. In Matthew 28, Jesus instructs his disciples to go to an appointed place on a mountain outside of Galilee. As they gather, they see Jesus, and their immediate response to him is to worship. Jesus spent the better part of his earthly ministry pouring himself into and mentoring these disciples. The relationship they share with Jesus is built upon daily time with him, nurturing their friendship, learning about faith, witnessing his miracles, praying together, learning about the coming Holy Spirit, listening to his word, suffering together, and watching Jesus's relationship with his father.

That's not all. The writer of Hebrews puts into perspective the role relationship has to suffering in the heart of Jesus:

> We do see Jesus, who was made lower than the angels for a little while, now crowned with glory and honor because he suffered death, so that by the grace of God he might taste death for everyone. In bringing many sons and daughters to glory, it was fitting that God, for whom and through whom everything exists, should make the pioneer of their salvation perfect through what he suffered.
>
> —HEBREWS 2:9–10

So what is next for the worshiper? How is the worshiper able to respond with perseverance when under pressure to throw up their hands and quit?

Worshipers of the most high God are absolutely committed to the long game. Each moment of suffering provides the worshiper opportunity to refine, build, strengthen, edify, and encourage their relationship with Jesus. And as they learn the joy of persevering, they are able to enjoy the spiritual formation process that promotes an active, engaging, and enriching relationship with Jesus. Their worship of Christ serves as the platform for living above the cares and distractions of this ungodly, selfish culture. The apostle Paul gives great encouragement and advice for those seeking the way of worship:

Persevering

Therefore we do not lose heart. Though outwardly we are wasting away, yet inwardly we are being renewed day by day. For our light and momentary troubles are achieving for us an eternal glory that far outweighs them all. So we fix our eyes not on what is seen, but on what is unseen, since what is seen is temporary, but what is unseen is eternal.

—2 CORINTHIANS 4:16–18

CHAPTER 28

PROCESS

"Okay everybody, we have reason to celebrate Anastasia today. She has successfully completed her journey as an apprentice and so shall be knighted a full-fledged guide this weekend!" John shouted.

Anastasia beamed as we clapped and cheered.

"Does this mean I don't have to take orders from you anymore?" she asked playfully.

"Nice try. I still sign your paycheck. Just because you're a guide doesn't mean you stop learning, young one."

We coasted gently down our last one hundred yards of river. The sun descended behind the canyon walls, and the air cooled. I drank it in as we crossed the calm waters to the takeout. It was a day forever etched in my soul.

As we made our way across the gentle current, the grey-haired, bearded sage we met at the beginning of our trip was waiting with the van and trailer. He smiled and waved at us as we arrived.

"How'd we do, guys?" His low raspy voice asked as he pulled our raft up onto the clay beach.

"Awesome!"

"Incredible!"

"A day I'll never forget!" We all responded in concert.

"Good, good. Now head on up to the van. There are warm cookies and various drinks to help you celebrate."

"That's what I'm talkin' about!" Neal guffawed.

John jumped out and walked up to the man and hugged him.

"So are you guys related?" I asked.

"Oh yeah, meet Big John, my dad. He's a legend . . . in his own mind," our guide said as he patted him on the shoulder.

"Not a legend, just old," the sage replied.

As father and son gathered our gear and began loading the van, a rugged, faded-red Jeep CJ-7 blaring classic rock flew into the gravel clearing near us. A lanky, curly-headed young man jumped out.

"You guys need some help?" he asked exuberantly.

"Frankie!" John went over and gave him a bear hug, then introduced me to him. "This is Michael from Nashville. He killed it today." The young man shook my hand and immediately engaged me in conversation as John kept working.

"Nashville, the stuff of country legends, man. I'm a huge Johnny Cash fan," he said.

"Yeah, we love living there. It seems like you guys have your own legends around here." I looked toward John and his dad.

"Totally. It's incredible to learn from these guys. They are river royalty. You were in the raft with the very best today."

"Yeah, this was a day I'll never forget," I said.

"It will be quite a while before I can read the river like they do. It's like the waters are in them or something. They are Jedi!"

"I'm sure you'll get there. Everything is a process, right?"

"You got that right. Big John always tells us to keep the long view in mind. Each stage has its competencies and evaluations you have to pass. Once you're accepted into the program, you go from apprentice to guide, guide to master guide. From there, it's on to mentor guide. That means you are really multiplying yourself, training up other guides. Beyond that, I suppose it is just legendary status, and you can't really measure that." Frankie glanced over to Big John as he worked. "The amazing thing is, the greatest legend of them all, the dude that has run more water and saved more lives than anyone, baked you cookies and is loading up your gear. Let that sink in! Being a legend isn't what you think."

I considered everything the gregarious outdoorsman said. In that moment, I found myself juxtaposing his statements over my own career in music as a songwriter, artist, and worship leader. I was just beginning. Could I be patient enough to let the process do its work in my life?

Every time you cross my mind, I break out in exclamations of thanks to God. Each exclamation is a trigger to prayer. I find myself praying for you with a glad heart. I am so pleased that you have continued on in this with us, believing and proclaiming God's Message, from the day you heard it right up to the present. There has never been the slightest doubt in my mind that the God who started this great work in you would keep at it and bring it to a flourishing finish on the very day Christ Jesus appears.

—PHILIPPIANS 1:3–6 MSG

The way of worship is the journey of a lifetime. It is a process filled with joy, sorrow, struggle, and victory. Not only is God finishing the work he started in us, but we are growing in our faith, our calling, and our craft. We have been adopted into the family by his grace, called and set apart to make disciples and lead people to fully worship their Savior. We are on our way. With every Scripture passage studied, every class attended, every service planned, every song written, every production executed, every meeting held, every book read, every coffee with a mentor or mentee; through every stage and every season, marriage and singleness, friendship and parenting, we are being shaped in the way of worship.

I loved the beauty of discipleship, succession, and process that was modeled in the rafting company. The way of the river guides was not only to allow the process to work in them individually, to become the most developed version of themselves, but also to give away their knowledge and wisdom to those coming up.

In an age of instant information and gratification, our tendency is to want the privileges without the process. Let's face it; sometimes we want the authority and gravitas of a master without the years of hard work it takes to become one.

There are no shortcuts to becoming a master of anything. God's timetable is not our timetable. Trust the process. Like Big John always said, "Keep the long view in mind."

The "river" has called you to experience the power and beauty of the waters of life. You have been chosen and set apart to not only experience the transcendent beauty of God yourself but to help others do the same. This is the way of worship.

The passage from Philippians 1 above is exactly the kind of exhortation worshipers need when coming to the end of a study like we've just completed. I dearly love the way Philippians 1:6 is translated in the New King James Version:

Being confident of this very thing, that He who has begun a good work in you will complete it until the day of Jesus Christ.

—PHILIPPIANS 1:6 NKJV

God is the one beginning and completing his work in each and every worshiper. God is shaping and transforming us for the way of worship. God is in the process of perfecting you and me for the way of worship! He is completing his good work in us so that we will be conformed and transformed into his image. God is in the process of preparing our hearts for kingdom ministry.

Preparing Our Hearts

Before actually placing your hand in the water, grabbing an oar, and starting to row with a team of worshipers on this river of life, it is important that we go through the process of preparation. God wants all hearts prepared and equipped for the task of living and leading worship. It is important to remember that God is the one who prepares each person for the task. And this type of preparation is a lifelong process.

The apostle Peter, in writing his epistle, reminds the older saints that they are to nurture and edify the younger leaders in ministry. He then turns his attention to exhorting those that are younger in ministry. He concludes this process by saying,

> And the God of all grace, who called you to his eternal glory in Christ, after you have suffered a little while, will himself restore you and make you strong, firm and steadfast.
> —1 PETER 5:10

Here, the great apostle outlines the process of preparation, including the very points of spiritual formation, necessary for the way of worship.

He Perfects

God is in the process of perfecting you and me. He wants to refine, hone, improve, and sharpen our abilities and talents and, in the process, faithfully develop our skills for his glory.

His sweet, precious Holy Spirit is actively working in each of us. As we faithfully seek God's direction, counsel, and guidance, he actively conforms us to his image, tempers our dispositions, smooths out any rough areas in our personalities, gives us a vision for ministry, and implants in our hearts a desire to worship. It takes time for God to perfect us, and the process is never fully completed in this life. Even so, he is the one who perfects and completes until the day he calls us to heaven.

Sometimes, he perfects us in areas where we are most vulnerable, self-conscious, and insecure. At other times, he perfects us in areas where we seem the most confident and self-assured. All in all, he works at shaping our lives so that we can be confident that he will do his good work in us.

He Establishes

God is also in the process of establishing—privately and in public, personally and professionally. In so doing, God proves, confirms, and verifies us and our work, all for his glory. The psalmist makes this request of the Lord:

> May the favor of the LORD our God rest on us; establish the work
> of our hands for us—yes, establish the work of our hands.
> —PSALM 90:17

When God establishes our work, he exalts and vindicates our efforts. He brings success. He demonstrates his favor upon all we do. This is where we learn how to delight in the provisions of our Lord. We don't have to be worried by the pressure to succeed or the rat race to the top. Success and getting everything done becomes a Holy Spirit activity. Again, look at the process:

> All of you, clothe yourselves with humility toward one another, because,

"God opposes the proud
but shows favor to the humble."

Humble yourselves, therefore, under God's mighty hand, that he
may lift you up in due time.

—1 PETER 5:5–6

This is where (and why) humbling ourselves *under the mighty hand of God* is most important. God resists the proud and gives grace to the humble. As you and I submit, clothe ourselves, and humble ourselves before God, at just the right time, he will begin his work in our hearts and complete it in his own time.

Why this kind of process? So that he will get the credit. When we experience any measure of success, our first and greatest temptation is to brag about the things we can do, say, and build. It's so easy for us to ignore the truth that God is the one who brings success. In the process, we become boastful. All of us deal with this temptation. And for some reason, those of us charged with the responsibility of leading worship seem to be the most vulnerable in this area. God's good timing and slow process helps protect us from that danger.

He Strengthens

God strengthens us to carry out ministry in the power of the Holy Spirit. When the Holy Spirit strengthens, he reinforces spiritual graces, fortifies the ability to resist the evil one, and intensifies spiritual insights. And he strengthens us in every way.

Intellectually, he gives us insight, wisdom, articulation, courage, and words of encouragement.

Physically, he makes all of us stronger, provides endurance for the journey, and sustains our health along the way.

Emotionally, he brings peace, rest, comfort, solitude, and affirmation during times of struggle.

Mentally, he grants abilities to comprehend, remember details, and recall concepts.

Educationally, we learn how to lead and follow, being equipped to stand and lead with confidence.

Spiritually, he gives grace for success, faith to believe, the ability to resist temptation, and vision for tomorrow.

He Settles

What does it mean for God to "settle" us? I like to think of it like being told to "*chill*, calm down, and relax." The final area of preparation involves resting in the presence of the Lord.

It's so easy for us to get all stirred up and anxious about the uncertainties we all face. God is the one who *settles our spirit*. He alone is the one who brings peace to an anxious heart. God has no intention of telling us to stop doing what he calls us to do. But he does want us to rest in him.

Remember his promises and process—performed by his sweet, precious Holy Spirit—is to perfect, establish, strengthen, and settle . . . you. Allow God to calm your spirit. Remember, as a worshiper committed to the way of worship, Jesus is our peace, contentment, and consolation always!

EPILOGUE

Worship is the submission of all of our nature to God. It is the quickening of the conscience by his holiness; the nourishment of mind with his truth; the purifying of imagination by his beauty; the opening of the heart to his love; the surrender of will to his purpose—all this gathered up in adoration, the most selfless emotion of which our nature is capable.

—WILLIAM TEMPLE

What an adventure we had that day. I had no idea that one day on the river in Colorado with our guide, John, his apprentice, Anastasia, and the hilarious couple from New York would still be inspiring over twenty years later. It reminds me how the power and presence of God comes to us. Just moments in his presence, in his Word, brings an endless fountain, a river flowing to and through our thirsty souls, inspiring David to say, "Better is one day in Your house . . ."

This is a lifelong journey. I've been singing, playing, writing, and worshiping in my local church since I was seven years old—thirty years now. I can say this: every season of life has been marked by his goodness and mercy. From mountaintops to the deep, long valleys, God is more real to me now than ever. Through excruciating loss, failure, and defeat, victories and peace, I'm filled with more hope and gratitude than ever.

The beauty of our God is inexhaustible, higher, farther, and greater than we could ever discover or describe. The way of worship is a way of adventure, exploration, discovery, peace, beauty, struggle, victory, and hope. We become like what or whom we worship. As we move deeper into the worship of Jesus, we become more like him; we discover who we are meant to be. We are saved, healed, and transformed for all eternity as our hearts learn to fully worship Jesus with surrendered awe. We are enthroning the only One worthy of our full passion and pursuit. In that process, we are changed to be free from lesser things and given to serve others wholeheartedly. When we give ourselves away to him and to others, that is when we really discover who we were created to be.

The river of life is alive! He is moving and working among us, and my greatest joy is to not only respond to his revelation with full-hearted worship but to help others do the same. To be a "gospel-pointer" is the greatest joy of my life. As worship guides, we help people experience who they were made for: the river of life.

The way of worship is what we were created for. It is the path of deepening our relationship with the Most High, the Savior of our souls. The way of worship is the activity of heaven. We join the multitude of souls and created beings already experiencing his perfection in eternity, and with our lives we join the seraphim, the burning ones, singing, "Holy, holy, holy is the Lord God Almighty, who was and is, and is to come." The way of worship is the journey of responding to all God is, says, and does. This way calls us not only to respond upward in praise and adoration, inward in deep and abiding surrender and devotion, but also outward in humble service to others. If I could leave you with one thing, these words of Jesus sum it up:

"Do you understand what I have done for you?" he asked them.
"You call me 'Teacher' and 'Lord,' and rightly so, for that is what I am.

Now that I, your Lord and Teacher, have washed your feet, you also should wash one another's feet. I have set you an example that you should do as I have done for you. Very truly I tell you, no servant is greater than his master, nor is a messenger greater than the one who sent him. Now that you know these things, you will be blessed if you do them."

—JOHN 12:13–17

This has been an amazing journey together. Michael's ability to tell the story is always incredible to me. The metaphor reminds me of how deeply personal our relationship with Jesus is. Over these last twenty-eight chapters, we have unpacked numerous principles that speak to the heart of those seeking the way of worship. In the final analysis, we learned that there is a five-fold outcome when one diligently seeks the way of worship.

First, the way of worship is formational. The Holy Spirit takes our own dynamic walk in heartfelt worship with Christ and uses it as an opportunity to mold, fashion, and shape us into his image. This is a gradual formation that takes place every time we feast on the Word of God, worship the God of the Word, and understand more fully the application of his Word on our lives.

Second, the way of worship is transformational. God is in the process of changing us from old to new. God is in the transformation business. He changes people. As we teach, train, encourage, edify, and share the gospel, the Holy Spirit transforms our lives from dead to living, and from hurting and broken to healed and restored. God takes us as broken, self-serving worshipers and transforms us into worshipers of the most high God.

Third, the way of worship is relational. Our worship is driven by relationships, both horizontal and vertical: our relationship to God and our relationships to the people around us. God is all about relationships. God desires to *be with us.* He desires relationship. Our relationship with God should enable us to establish, build, shape, cultivate, and enjoy relationship with believers all around us. When it's all been said and done—when we have led our final worship set, and God has called us home to glory—people will remember more about the relationship we had with them than anything else. They will recall the times we were kind, gracious, loving, and accepting. They will remember us for who and what we are more than anything else.

Fourth, the way of worship is missional. The intent and application of *missional* to our own daily living reaches far past the novelty and triteness of language. Our mission, our calling, is to carry the gospel to a lost and dying world. Those seeking the way of worship become the hands and feet of Jesus. They are driven by passion for God and love for others. Obedience to that mission is driven by a deep love for Jesus.

Fifth, the way of worship is reproducible. Our goal is to promote and bring into the body of Christ, the church, citizens from every tribe, tongue, culture, nation, and people group. Why? So that they can become worshipers too! Bringing others into the worship community may become one of the most rewarding parts of worship and worship leading. Contextualization becomes reality as we continually learn how to relate our message to culture.

You then, my son, be strong in the grace that is in Christ Jesus. And the things you have heard me say in the presence of many witnesses entrust to reliable people who will also be qualified to teach others.

—2 TIMOTHY 2:1–2

ACKNOWLEDGMENTS

FROM MICHAEL

I must acknowledge those who have shaped me in the way of worship. My wife Leah has loved me with an unwavering grace and her unrelenting passion for the Lord and his Word inspires me to the core. God has used her to express his love and beauty to me in countless ways on the journey. I'm forever grateful. My children, Micah, Maisie, and Wyatt, are like facets of a precious diamond, each reflecting a unique and stunning view of God at work. Being their father is the greatest gift I could think of.

My parents, Bob and Bonnie Neale, raised me in safe and loving home where the Word of God was memorized and where praises were sung daily around the piano and in our church life. They paved the way of worship for me, living faithful lives of love, service, and worship.

Finally, there is my friend, brother, teacher, and mentor Vernon Whaley, without whom this book would not be possible. Vernon's wisdom, tenacity, vision, humility, faithfulness, and heart for Jesus has been an endless well of encouragement to me and the thousands of students he has equipped through the universities and ministries he has served. I'm so thankful he decided to write this book with me, and I'm even more thankful to call him friend and prayer partner on the way of worship.

FROM VERNON

I too wish to acknowledge those who have shaped me in the way of worship. First, my wife, Beth, has bestowed upon me unconditional love for more than forty-seven years. Over the years, God has provided for us a platform for knowing and loving his word and work on so many levels. She is my rock! Sometimes I refer to Beth as the "holy spirit in a skirt." Her insight, wisdom, love for people, and love for the Lord has helped make our marriage strong and enduring. Our children, Laurie Roe (with her Jeremy) and Jeremy (with his Kenya), make parenting adult children an enriching and joyful experience. Then there are our six grandchildren: Carter, Luca, Noah, Daisy, Eliza, and Aliyanna are the best any Papa could hope for. I get to spoil them pretty much all the time.

My parents, D. L. "Lee" and Ethel Whaley, taught me early how to live a life of faith, fully trusting God when the road ahead was not always clear. Beth's parents, Rolla and Agnes Smith, taught us the joy of consistency of character. Our dads were pastors, and our homes were always blessed with guests; evangelists, missionaries, and pastors were a big part of our life. Both sets of parents are with the Lord now, but their individual and collective influence have shaped us so that today we are thoroughly committed to the way of worship as a lifestyle.

Finally, there is my friend, brother, and fellow musician Michael Neale. Thank you for giving me this opportunity to write with you. You are without a doubt one of the best storytellers ever. You write with such an engaging spirit. Your gift of prose is one of your strongest qualities as a songwriter and worship leader. I too am thankful to the Lord for the opportunity to write this book together. And I'm grateful that through this process with have become life-long worshiping comrades.

FROM MICHAEL AND VERNON

The pastors that we have worked and served with over the years have each, in their own way, left indelible marks on our character and how we think about God. Their leadership and shepherding have been vital on our journey as husbands, fathers, leaders, creators, and most importantly, worshipers. For Michael: Tom Mullins, Todd Mullins, John Maxwell, Bob Neale, Gary Powell, Jack Graham, Jarrett Stephens, and many others "have championed my life and leadership, and I'm forever grateful." For Vernon: Eugene Waddell, Dr. Melvin Worthington, Joe Grizzle, Robert Morgan, Dr. Ted Traylor, Dr. Ron Hawkins, Dr. Doug Randlett, Dr. John Kinchen, and Dr. Paul Rumrill have encouraged and prayed over my life and ministry for years. I am eternally grateful for their lives of example and influence.

Over the years, both of us have been privileged to work with skilled, Holy Spirit–filled artists, songwriters, orchestrators, arrangers, and producers on a level seldom afforded to church musicians.

I (Michael) have had the privilege of working with many artists and leaders in the church through the years, but none have impacted my view of my role in the way of worship more than my good friend Paul Baloche. Paul has led millions to the throne of Jesus in worship with his songs and faithful pastoral service through the years. His personal mentorship came to me at exactly the right time. His humble way of publicly and privately communing with God while helping others do the same, set me on the right path as both a worshiper and a leader of worshipers. His impact on me has been immeasurable.

I (Vernon) have been influenced by scores of men and women.

But In recent years I've had opportunity to work alongside singer-songwriter Al Denson. His unselfishness and life of selfless service has inspired me on so many levels. He loves Jesus. And his love for the Lord impacts the way he loves people. I am personally beholden to Al's mentorship and Holy Spirit inspired encouragement.

Verne Kenney, our agent on this project, was the chief door-opener and a wonderful advisor. His partnership in helping us see this through was much needed. Thank you. Thank you.

Ryan Pazdur, Matthew Estel, and the entire team at Zondervan are so wonderful to work with. We are deeply grateful for their belief in this project and all they do to equip the body of Christ with incredible resources.

"The hand that steers the stars and turns the pages of history is the same that arranges our days and bestows the grace needed for each one."

NOTES

Introduction

1. "In the same day made a covenant with Abram, saying, unto thy seed have I given this land, from the river of Egypt unto the great river, the river Euphrates" (Gen 15:18).
2. "And when she could no longer hide him, she took for him an ark of bulrushes, and daubed it with slime and with pitch, and put the child therein; and she laid it in the flags by the river's brink" (Exod 2:3).
3. "Behold, he drinketh up a river, and hasteth not: he trusteth that he can draw up Jordan into his mouth" (Job 40:23 KJV).
4. "He shall be like a tree planted by the rivers of water that bringeth forth its fruit in its season" (Ps 1:3 KJV). They shall be abundantly satisfied with the fatness of thy house; and thou shalt make them drink of the river of thy pleasures" (Ps 36:8 KJV).

   "There is a river, the streams whereof shall make glad the city of Elohim, the holy place of the tabernacles of the most High" (Ps 46:4 KJV).
5. "For he shall be as a tree planted by the waters, and that spreadeth out her roots by the river, and shall not see when heat cometh, but her leaf shall be green; and shall not be careful in the year of drought, neither shall cease from yielding fruit" (Jer 17:8). "And I saw in a vision; and it came to pass, when I saw, that I was at Shushan in the palace, which is in the province of Elam; and I saw in a vision, and I was by the river of Ulai" (Dan 8:2). "Then I lifted up mine eyes, and saw, and, behold,

there stood before the river a ram which had two horns: and the two horns were high; but one was higher than the other, and the higher came up last" (Dan 8:3 KJV).

6. "Then Jesus came from Galilee to John at the Jordan to be baptized by him" (Matt 3:13).

7. "If anyone thirsts, let him come to Me and drink. He who believe in Me, as the Scripture has said, "out of his heart will flow rivers of living water." But this He spoke concerning the Spirit, whom those believing in Him would receive" (John 7:37–39 NKJV).

8. "And there went out unto him all the land of Judaea, and they of Jerusalem, and were all baptized of him in the river of Jordan, confessing their sins" (Mark 1:5 NKJV).

9. "And on the sabbath we went out of the city by a river side, where prayer was wont to be made; and we sat down, and spake unto the women which resorted thither" (Acts 16:13 KJV).

10. "And he shewed me a pure river of water of life, clear as crystal, proceeding out of the throne of and of the Lamb" (Rev 22:1 KJV).

Chapter 1: His Plan

1. C. S. Lewis, *Reflections on the Psalms* (London: Harcourt Brace, 1958).

Chapter 5: Spirit and Truth

1. John Piper, *Desiring God: Meditations of a Christian Hedonist* (Colorado Springs: Multnomah, 1986).

2. Dallas Willard, "Personal Soul Care," *Dallas Willard*, 2006, http://www.dwillard.org/articles/individual/personal-soul-care (accessed May 1, 2019).

Chapter 6: His Word

1. Martin Luther, *Christian Liberty* (Philadelphia: Lutheran Publication Society, 1903), 8.

2. Ronald E. Hawkins, personal interview by Vernon M. Whaley with Dr. Ronald E. Hawkins, March 28, 2019.

3. Ronald E. Hawkins, personal interview by Vernon M. Whaley with Dr. Ronald E. Hawkins, March 28, 2019.

4. Simon W. Blackburn, "Truth," *Encyclopedia Britannica*, https://www.britannica.com/topic/truth-philosophy-and-logic (accessed May 10, 2019).

Chapter 8: Time

1. "Definition of Time," *Exactly What Is . . . Time?* 2019, http://www.exactly whatistime.com/definition-of-time/ (accessed May 20, 2019).
2. "Definition of Time."
3. "Definition of Time."
4. Frances Havergal, *Take My Life and Let It Be*; see https://www.christ ianity.com/church/church-history/timeline/1801–1900/frances -havergal-wrote-take-my-life-and-let-it-be-11630571.html (accessed May 20, 2019).
5. David Wilkerson, *Spending Time with Jesus*, available at http://www .sermonindex.net/modules/newbb/viewtopic.php?topic_id=53667& forum=45 (accessed May 20, 2019).
6. Wilkerson, *Spending Time with Jesus.*
7. William M. Runyan, *Lord, I Have Shut the Door,* "Favorite Hymns of Praise. Hymn 99," *Hymnary.org* (Chicago: Tabernacle, 1923), https:// hymnary.org/hymn/fhop/page/99 (accessed May 20, 2019).
8. Oswald Chambers, *My Utmost for His Highest* (New York: Dodd, Mead, 1935), August 23.
9. "Strong's 61805—*exagorazo,*" *Blue Letter Bible,* https://www.blueletter bible.org/lang/lexicon/lexicon.cfm?Strongs=G1805&t=NKJV (accessed May 20, 2019).
10. Chambers, *My Utmost for His Highest,* August 23.

Chapter 9: Character

1. "Character," *Dictionary.com,* https://www.dictionary.com/browse/character (accessed July 27, 2019).
2. Brett McKay and Kate McKay, *A Man's Life, Character, On Manhood, On Virtue,* June 25, 2013, last updated November 17, 2018, https://www .artofmanliness.com/articles/what-is-character-its-3-true-qualities -and-how-to-develop-it/ (accessed May 24, 2019).
3. Cited in McKay and McKay, *Man's Life.*
4. S. Michael Houdmann, *"Christian Character—What Does the Bible Say?"* Got Questions Ministry, https://www.compellingtruth.org/Christian -character.html (accessed May 24, 2019).
5. Jim Dailey, "Developing Christ Like Character," August 30, 2012, *Billy Graham Evangelistic Association,* https://billygraham.org/story /developing-christlike-character (accessed May 24, 2019).

6. Jill Schoenberg, "What Is Good Character?" *Journal Buddies*, https://www.journalbuddies.com/teacher-parent-resources/what-is-good-character/ (accessed May 24, 2019).

7. "The Importance of Character," *Truth or Tradition?*, https://www.truthortradition.com/articles/the-importance-of-character (accessed May 24, 2019).

8. William Straton Bruce, *The Formation of Christian Character*, originally published in 1908 and quoted in https://www.artofmanliness.com/articles/what-is-character-its-3-true-qualities-and-how-to-develop-it/ (accessed May 24, 2019).

9. "The Importance of Character."

10. Barrie Davenport, "20 Good Character Traits Essential for Happiness," *Live Bold & Bloom*, https://liveboldandbloom.com/10/relationships/good-character-traits (accessed May 22, 2019).

11. "Fear of the Lord," *Daily Bread*, September 20, 1992, http://www.sermonillustrations.com/a-z/f/fear_of_god.htm (accessed July 27, 2019).

12. Charles R. Swindoll, "J.P. Morgan, quoted in Warren Wiersbe, Making Sense of the Ministry," *Swindoll's Ultimate Book of Illustrations and Quotes* (Nashville: Thomas Nelson, 1998), 66.

Chapter 10: Fresh Encounters

1. Oswald Chambers, *My Utmost for His Highest: Devotional Journal* (Grand Rapids: Discovery House, 1992), May 26. Available at https://utmost.org/thinking-of-prayer-as-jesus-taught/ (accessed May 26, 2019).

Chapter 11: Brokenness

1. A. W. Tozer, *The Root of Righteousness* (Camp Hill, PA: Christian Publications, 1986), 137.

2. Mildred Witte Struven, *Bits and Pieces*, September 19, 1991, 6.

3. Harold Vaughan, "Brokenness: A Little Understood and Lightly Esteemed Virtue," *Christ Life Ministries*, http://www.christlifemin.org/home/blog/articles/brokenness-a-little-understood-and-lightly-esteemed-virtue/ (accessed May 27, 2019).

4. Vaughan, "Brokenness."

5. Vaughan, "Brokenness."

6. Chambers, *My Utmost for His Highest*, August 22.

Chapter 12: Humility

1. Andrew Murray, *Humility: The Beauty of Holiness* (London: Nisbet, 1896), 94.
2. Strong's Concordance H6065, *Blue Letter Bible*, https://www.blueletter bible.org/lang/lexicon/lexicon.cfm?Strongs=H6035&t=NKJV (accessed May 29, 2019).
3. Strong's Concordance H6065, *Blue Letter Bible*, https://www.blueletter bible.org/lang/lexicon/lexicon.cfm?Strongs=H6035&t=NKJV (Accessed May 29, 2019).
4. https://www.blueletterbible.org/search/search.cfm?Criteria=Humble&t =NKJV#s=s_primary_0_1 (accessed May 29, 2019).
5. Strong's Concordance G5013, *Blue Letter Bible*. https://www.blueletter bible.org/lang/lexicon/lexicon.cfm?Strongs=G5013&t=NKJV (Accessed May 29, 2019).
6. Strong's Concordance G5013.
7. "Humble," *Webster's Dictionary*, 1913, available at https://www.webster -dictionary.org/definition/humble (accessed May 29, 2019).
8. "Humble," *Webster's Dictionary*.
9. James Packer, *Your Father Loves You* (London: Harold Shaw, 1986).
10. Darlene Zschech, "The Humility to Worship the Lord," Revival Ministries International, https://www.revival.com/a/2429-the-humility-to-worship -the-lord (accessed May 30, 2019).
11. C. S. Lewis, *Mere Christianity* (New York: Macmillan, 1952), 109.

Chapter 13: Integrity

1. Dave Anderson "The Vital Difference between Integrity and Character," *Dave Anderson's LearnToLead*, http://blog.learntolead.com/archives/tag/the -vital-difference-between-character-and-integrity/ (accessed May 30, 2019).
2. "I-35W Mississippi River Bridge," *Wikipedia: The Free Encyclopedia*, Wikimedia Foundation, May 29, 2019, http://en.wikipedia.org/wiki /I-35W_Mississippi_River_Bridge (accessed July 27, 2019).
3. Oswald Chambers, *My Utmost for His Highest: Devotional Journal* (Grand Rapids: Discovery House, 1992), May 25, available at https://utmost .org/classic/the-test-of-self-interest-classic/ (accessed May 27, 2019).
4. Pamela Rose Williams, "Bible Verses about Integrity: 20 Important Scripture Quotes," *What Christians Want to Know*, https://www.what christianswanttoknow.com/bible-verses-about-integrity-20-important -scripture-quotes/ (accessed May 30, 2019).

Chapter 14: Living Water

1. "John 7:37–39 Commentary," *Precept Austin*, December 28, 2012, https://www.preceptaustin.org/john_737-39_commentary (accessed May 28, 2019).

2. "Strong's G1372," *Blue Letter Bible*, https://www.blueletterbible.org/lang/lexicon/lexicon.cfm?Strongs=G1372&t=NKJV (accessed May 28, 2019).

3. "πιστεύω = *pisteúō*," *Blue Letter Bible*, https://www.blueletterbible.org/lang/lexicon/lexicon.cfm?Strongs=G4100&t=NKJV (accessed May 29, 2019).

4. "Strong's G2198," *Blue Letter Bible*, https://www.blueletterbible.org/lang/lexicon/lexicon.cfm?Strongs=G2198&t=NKJV (accessed May 29, 2019).

5. Ray Pritchard, "When God Comes Near: 'I Believe in the Holy Spirit,'" *Keep Believing Ministries*, May 16, 2004, http://www.keepbelieving.com/sermon/2004-05-16-When-God-Comes-Near-I-Believe-in-the-Holy-Spirit/ (accessed May 29, 2019).

6. Douglas Cecil, "The Age-Old Question . . . Are You Thirsty?," *Precept Austin*, updated December 28, 2018, https://www.preceptaustin.org/john_737-39_commentary (accessed May 29, 2019).

7. Ken Boa, "John 4:1–15 Commentary," *Precept Austin*, https://www.preceptaustin.org/index.php/john_44-15_commentary (accessed May 29, 2019).

8. Oswald Chambers, "Fountains of Blessings," *My Utmost for His Highest: Devotional Journal*, ed. James Reimann (September 7, 1991).

9. Chambers, "Fountains of Blessings."

10. Dan Graves, "Augustine of Hippo (354–430 AD), in *Confessions*," quoted in "Article #15," *Christian History Institute*, https://christianhistoryinstitute.org/incontext/article/augustine (accessed May 29, 2019).

Chapter 15: Generosity

1. "Generosity," *Vocabulary.com*, https://www.vocabulary.com/dictionary/generosity (accessed June 3, 2019).

2. "Generosity," Dictionary.com, https://www.dictionary.com/browse/generosity (accessed June 3. 2019).

3. "Generosity," Dictionary.com.

4. Quoted at "Generosity Quotes," *GoodReads*, https://www.goodreads.com/quotes/tag/generosity (accessed June 3, 2019).

5. Quoted at Stephen Dela Cruz, "10 of the Most Powerful Generosity Quotes and Why You Need Them," *Medium*, February 18, 2017, https://medium.com/the-beta-mode/10-of-the-most-powerful-generosity-quotes-and-why-you-need-them-37759c9373b.

6. Paul E. Chapman, "Four Types of Biblical Giving You Should Practice This Week," *PaulEChapman.com*, March 28, 2017, https://paulechapman.com/2017/03/28/four-types-of-biblical-giving-you-should-practice-this-week/ (accessed June 3, 2019).

7. Randy Alcorn, "What Are the Four Types of Bible Giving?," *FaithPro.org*, https://faithpro.org/what-are-the-four-types-of-bible-giving/ (accessed June 3, 2019).

8. Chapman, "Four Types of Biblical Giving."

Chapter 16: Equipping

1. Equip = *katartizo* (from *katá* = with + *artízō* = to adjust, fit, finish, in turn from *ártios* = fit, complete) means to fit or join together and so to mend or repair. Strong's 2675. *Precept Austin*, https://www.preceptaustin.org/hebrews_1320–21 (accessed June 4, 2019).

2. Ray Stedman, "Hebrews 13:20–21 Commentary," *Precept Austin*, October 24, 2016, https://www.preceptaustin.org/hebrews_1320–21 (accessed June 4, 2019).

3. Charles Spurgeon, "Hebrews 13:20–21 Commentary," *Precept Austin*, October 24, 2016, https://www.preceptaustin.org/hebrews_1320–21 (accessed June 4, 2019).

4. Hiebert, "Hebrews 13:20–21 Commentary," *Precept Austin*, October 24, 2016, https://www.preceptaustin.org/hebrews_1320–21 (accessed June 4, 2019).

5. Ray Stedman, "Ephesians 4:12–13," *Precept Austin*, https://www.preceptaustin.org/ephesians_412–13.

6. Stedman, "Ephesians 4:12–13."

Chapter 17: Empowering

1. "Empower," *Lexico*, https://en.oxforddictionaries.com/definition/empower (accessed June 6, 2019).

2. "Empower."

3. "Strong's G1411," *Blue Letter Bible*, https://www.blueletterbible.org/lang/lexicon/lexicon.cfm?Strongs=G1411&t=KJV (accessed June 6, 2019).

4. Bezalel appears nine times in the NKJV of the Bible: Exod 31:1–9; 35:30–35; 36:1–2, 4, 8–38; 37; 38:22–23; 1 Chron 2:20; 2 Chron 1:5; and Ezra 10:30.

Chapter 18: Unifying

1. Definition of "unity" from the Cambridge Academic Content Dictionary, Cambridge University Press, https://dictionary.cambridge.org/us/dictionary/english/unity (accessed June 7, 2019).
2. "KJV Dictionary Definition: Unity," *AV1611*, https://av1611.com/kjbp/kjv-dictionary/unity.html (accessed June 7, 2019).
3. Belsan, "10 Bible Verses about Teamwork," *Teamwork Definition*, January 20, 2014, http://teamworkdefinition.com/quotesfromthebible/ (accessed June 7, 2019).
4. "Ephesians 4:2–3," *Precept Austin*, May 15, 2018, https://www.preceptaustin.org/ephesians_42-3 (accessed June 9, 2019).
5. J. A. Barnes, *Barnes NT Commentary*, "Ephesians 4:2–3 Commentary," *Precept Austin*, May 15, 2018, https://www.preceptaustin.org/ephesians_42-3 (accessed June 7, 2019).
6. Danker, "Ephesians 4:2–3 Commentary," *Precept Austin*, May 15, 2018, https://www.preceptaustin.org/ephesians_42-3 (accessed June 9, 2019).

Chapter 19: Serving

1. "Romans 12," *Blue Letter Bible*, https://www.blueletterbible.org/niv/rom/12/7/p0/t_conc_1058007 (accessed July 27, 2019).

Chapter 20: Sacrificing

1. Timothy Keller with Kathy Keller, *The Meaning of Marriage: Facing the Complexities of Commitment with the Wisdom of God* (New York: Penguin, 2011), 44.
2. Billy Graham, "Answers," *Billy Graham Evangelistic Association*, July 29, 2004, https://billygraham.org/answer/why-did-god-command-people-to-make-sacrifices-in-the-old-testament-when-they-wouldnt-completely-take-away-their-sins-like-jesus-sacrifice-did/ (accessed June 12, 2019).
3. Graham, "Answers."

Chapter 21: Craft

1. "Craft," *Merriam-Webster*, https://www.merriam-webster.com/dictionary/craft.

2. Nathan Isaacs, "Skill; Skilful," *Blue Letter Bible*, https://www.blue letterbible.org/search/Dictionary/viewTopic.cfm?topic=IT0008228 (accessed June 14, 2019).

3. Robert J. Morgan, "Interview with Cliff Barrows," October 29, 2017, in Vernon M. Whaley, *Exalt His Name Book 1* (Calumet City, IL: Evangelical Training Association, 2018), 95.

Chapter 22: Communication

1. Christian Eilers, "20+ Effective Communication Skills for Resumes & Workplace Success," *Zety*, June 5, 2019, https://zety.com/blog/comm unication-skills (accessed June 16, 2019).

2. Oswald Chambers, "Beware of Criticizing Others," *My Utmost for His Highest* (Grand Rapids: Discovery House, 1992), June 17.

3. Eilers, "20+ Effective Communication Skills."

Chapter 23: Confidence

1. "Strong's G3954," *Blue Letter Bible*, https://www.blueletterbible.org/lang /lexicon/lexicon.cfm?Strongs=G3954&t=NKJV (accessed July 27, 2019).

Chapter 24: Navigation

1. "What Is GPS?," *Garmin*, https://www8.garmin.com/aboutGPS/ (July 27, 2019).

2. David Guzik, "Letter to the Captives," *Blue Letter Bible Commentary*, 2015, https://www.blueletterbible.org/Comm/guzik_david/Study Guide2017-Jer/Jer-29.cfm (accessed June 21, 2019).

Chapter 25: Vision

1. "Two Ways to Study Worship with Me," *MysteryOfFaithBlog.com*, July 22, 2019, "What Does It Mean to Be a Prophetic Church?," February 6, 2017.

2. "Be Thou My Vision," trans. Mary E. Byrne, https://hymnary.org/text /be_thou_my_vision_o_lord_of_my_heart.

Chapter 26: Collaboration

1. "Collaborate," *Merriam-Webster*, https://www.merriam-webster.com /dictionary/collaborate (accessed on June 24, 2019).

2. "A Winning Combination: Collaborative Teamwork Equals Teamwork and Collaboration," *Smartsheet*, https://www.smartsheet.com/collaborative -teamwork (accessed June 24, 2019).

SCRIPTURE INDEX